Soft Paths

THE NATIONAL OUTDOOR LEADERSHIP SCHOOL

Soft Paths

◆

How to enjoy the wilderness without harming it

◆

Bruce Hampton and David Cole

Line drawings by Denise Casey

Stackpole Books

Published by
STACKPOLE BOOKS
Cameron and Kelker Streets
P.O. Box 1831
Harrisburg, PA 17105

Printed in the United States of America

10 9 8

Library of Congress Cataloging-in-Publication Data

Hampton, Bruce.
Soft paths: how to enjoy the wilderness without harming it / Bruce Hampton and David Cole.
p. cm.
Bibliography: p.
Includes index.
ISBN 0-8117-2234-1
1. Outdoor recreation—Environmental aspects.
2. Wilderness areas—Recreational use—Environmental aspects. I. Cole, David N.
II. Title.
GV191.66.H36 1988
333.78′4—dc19 88-2304
CIP

Contents

Acknowledgments

No single person can take credit for the practical conservation skills developed at the National Outdoor Leadership School. Rather, these techniques have evolved through constant refinement and improvement during the past twenty-three years, thanks to the efforts of the very best outdoor educators in the world. To these past and present NOLS instructors we gratefully dedicate this book.

Special thanks go to Jim Chisholm, Dave Chrislip, Lantien Chu, Molly Doran, Tim Easley, John Gans, Ian Gersten, John Gookin, Reb Gregg, Molly Hampton, John Hauf, Reese Jamison, Dave Kallgren, Ted Kerasote, Jonathan Kusel, Drew Leemon, Dave Neary, David Pekelney, Jim Ratz, and Mike Riley for their close reading of the text and thoughtful advice. Stephanie Kessler contributed material used in the chapter on bear country; Nancy Fitzsimmons and Rich Bloom provided information about coastal practices. Colorado Outward Bound contributed to the chapters on backcountry travel and rivers and lakes. Paul Calver, Sukey Richard, Will Waterman, and Tom Wright gave their careful attention to the design and format of this book.

The fine drawings of wilderness plants and animals are the work of Denise Casey, a talented Wyoming artist. Thanks also go to the Teton Science

School for use of the Murie Collection and to Tim Clark for his helpful critique.

We are grateful to the NOLS Board of Trustees for their encouragement, and particularly to Jim Ratz, NOLS Executive Director, for his vision and determination in bringing the advice and techniques found in these pages before the public eye. Finally, we owe lasting thanks to Paul Petzoldt, the founder of NOLS, who first taught us to care for wildlands and then showed us how to teach others.

Bruce Hampton
David Cole

November 1987

And what will be the disposition of the landscape?
Will it be used, as always, in whatever way we will,
or will it one day be accorded some dignity of its own?

—Barry Lopez, from *Arctic Dreams*

About This Book

When a Forest Service ranger encouraged us to publish the minimum-impact conservation techniques developed at the National Outdoor Leadership School, he advised: "You can't spell it out too simply for the average camper. Look how long we've had Smokey the Bear and Woodsy Owl warning people about fires and litter. Have careless people stopped burning down forests? Don't we still have litter in the backcountry? Aim your sights on the wilderness user who creates the mess for the rest of us."

These are not the harsh words of an elitist. They are the heartfelt frustrations of a dedicated land manager. Too many times had this ranger stood at trailheads handing out brochures describing conservation practices, only later to find them wadded up and trodden underfoot by a growing army of Vibram soles hiking the backcountry.

Like a worn-out parent dealing with an unruly child, the ranger was fed up with the behavior of the public toward its land. "Keep it basic," he admonished us. "Capitalize the rules, underline them, and then drive them home with a sledgehammer!"

But this book isn't like that at all. After twenty years of teaching outdoor skills and conservation techniques to students from all over the world, we at NOLS see the problem differently. Rules and regulations by themselves are not the answer.

Aldo Leopold, author of the classic *A Sand County Almanac*, questioned the effectiveness of regulation nearly forty years ago: "Obligations have no meaning without conscience, and the problem we face is the extension of the social conscience from people to land." Leopold knew it was not the place of government to lurk behind every tree, ready to spring upon the rule-breaker. Appropriate behavior flows from an understanding of and respect for the land, an inherent set of values within the individual user—a land ethic.

"But ethical behavior comes only with experience," our ranger friend argued, "and the problem is the well-meaning but inept user who can't seem to practice the simplest conservation techniques." In turn we ask: Don't all kinds of outdoor recreation have the problem of inexperienced participants? High standards of behavior are set by example. Examine the ethic of "clean climbing" for climbers or "catch and release" for fly-fishermen. How did a sophisticated level of ethical behavior spread throughout these popular sports in such a short time, reaching even beginners?

Our belief is that the answer to the problem flows from each backcountry user. Until we teach by way of personal example, there will be no cure for the abuse of our wildlands.

The following pages describe practical ways to reduce human impact in the backcountry—simple tools that everyone can use. Under each major topic, we discuss the rationale behind our recommended practices, based on the best scientific research on recreational impact. Readers will note that the words *wildland, backcountry,* and *wilderness* are used interchangeably; although most research and much of the terminology referred to in the text applies to designated wilderness in North America, our techniques apply to any remote recreation land throughout the world.

To provide authority for our suggestions, we have included a bibliography of the latest research. This field of study is new, however, and rapidly changing. We can't wait until all the answers are found, for meanwhile our backcountry continues to deteriorate. As in everyday life, decisions often have to be based on insufficient information. In this respect, these practices should be considered a "living document," evolving and changing as we learn more about the environment and our effect on it.

Practicing a wildland ethic implies wisdom gained from experience. In many ways, such wisdom may be the ultimate goal of responsible citizenry. The ranger's final question echoes off abused canyon floors and rumbles down eroded mountain trails: "Can we become good citizens before our remaining backcountry suffers irreparable harm?"

This book says, "yes." We at the National Outdoor Leadership School believe that outdoor recreationists are capable of practicing an ethic of individual responsibility toward our remaining wildlands. It is up to those of us who love our pristine backcountry to live this ethic and to spread its message to others. Nothing less will suffice if we want our wildlands to survive.

We have met the enemy and he is us.
—"Pogo," by Walt Kelly

Will Waterman

Chapter One

The Case for Minimum Impact

- During a single night, as many as a thousand people have camped in one valley of California's San Gorgonio Wilderness.
- Campsites in the Boundary Waters Canoe Area of Minnesota have suffered an 80 percent loss of vegetation.
- So many hikers have traversed the Old Bridle Path up New Hampshire's Mount Lafayette that the trail has eroded into a gully four feet deep, prompting trail crews to call it the "Old Bridle Trench."

In the Appalachians of Tennessee, the Baja desert of Mexico, the Sierra Nevada of California, even Alaska's remote coastline, the story is the same: User impact is spreading faster than land managers can control it. In the words of one frustrated researcher, "We are quite literally loving our wilderness to death."

Most of us have accepted the fact that we can never have the wilderness experiences of a Daniel Boone, Lewis and Clark, or John Wesley Powell. Nevertheless, we value the opportunity to visit those scenic and remote lands identified in the National Wilderness Preservation Act as places "where the earth and its community of life are untrammeled by man, where man himself is a visitor who does not remain."

Bill Petersen

Since 1965, recreational use of wilderness has grown by nearly 400 percent, resulting in impact not only to the environment but to the wilderness experience of visitors as well.

Between 1965 and 1980, recreational use of America's wilderness areas grew from slightly more than 4 million visitor-days (a twelve-hour stay by one person) to nearly 10 million per year. In 1984, our wilderness lands absorbed nearly 15 million visitor-days, up 50 percent since 1980, up 275 percent since 1965.

As the number of backcountry visitors grows, no longer are picking up litter and extinguishing matches good enough. For wilderness is more than just an unspoiled environment; it is a quality human experience demanding isolation. Thus, there are two dimensions to the problem of recreational impact—damage to the integrity of the land, and injury to the wilderness experience of others.

Solution by Default

In his book for climbers, *Basic Rockcraft*, Royal Robbins says, "A simple equation exists between freedom and numbers: the more people, the less freedom." Today, this maxim guides many public land managers in their attempt to balance backcountry recreation with protection of the wildland environment.

In a 1980 survey, researchers Randy Washburne and David Cole asked managers what they were doing to minimize impact problems. The National Park Service reported that nearly half of all parks allowed camping only in designated sites. Although National Forests, the Bureau of Land Management, and National Wildlife Refuges reported less restrictive actions, the trend in all agencies has been to regulate use. One need not look far for examples. Visitors to Linville Gorge Wilderness in North Carolina encounter a limit of thirty individuals per day. In Yellowstone National Park, users must obtain a permit before hiking the backcountry, and campsites are restricted. Only seven parties per day are allowed to launch on Idaho's Middle Fork of the Salmon River.

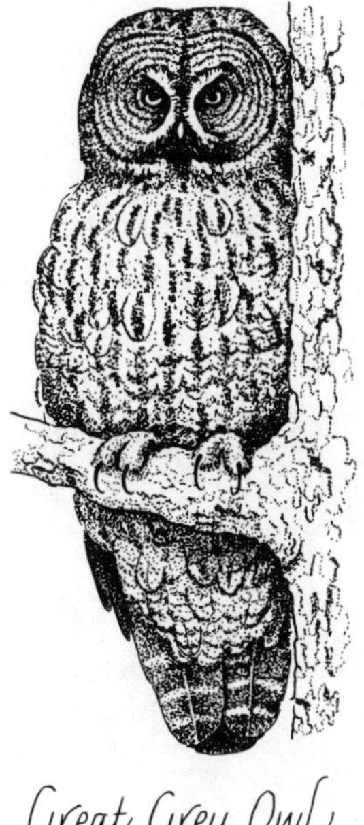
Great Grey Owl

Sometimes restrictions seem unavoidable. But often they come too late, after the damage is already done. No one who values wilderness wants to see these lands suffer more abuse. Yet is the only solution to tell users how to camp, where to camp, and how long to stay? Many of us, after all, seek the solitude and freedom of wildlands as temporary relief from a restrictive society.

We at NOLS believe that most damage is the result of visitors' unawareness of the consequences of their actions, not of malice. In fact, it would be difficult to find a more intelligent, more caring group of individuals; most backcountry users are anxious to do the right thing. Yet good intentions alone have fallen short.

The Path to a Wildland Ethic

Minimum-impact backcountry use is a hands-on, practical approach to caring about both the land and others who share its richness. Its success hinges on the willingness of the individual user to learn, to think, and then to commit knowledge to action. The resulting techniques are flexible and tempered by judgment and experience. They de-

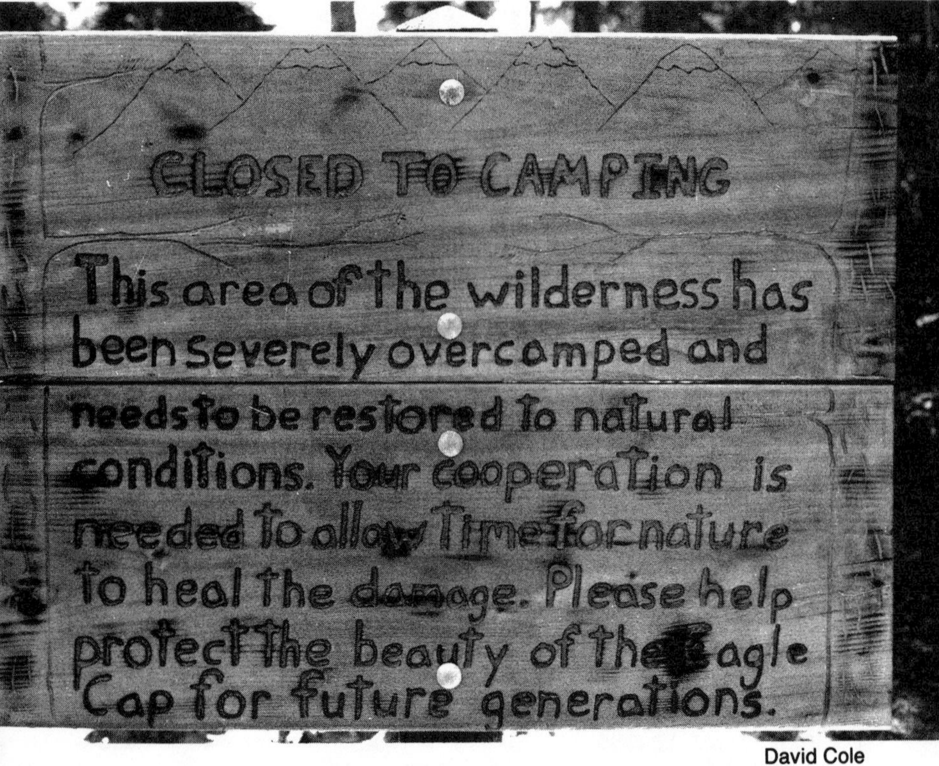

David Cole

Restrictions most often arrive after the damage is already done.

pend more on attitude and awareness than on rules and regulations. Minimum-impact practices don't replace one governmental set of rules with yet another.

"Rules are for fools," NOLS's founder Paul Petzoldt used to say. Paul wasn't advocating anarchy. He was reminding users that the most successful approach to a backcountry journey is for people to use their best judgment, not to follow blindly a set of rules.

Minimum-impact techniques are quick to adapt to changing conditions. Visitors must consider the variables of each place—soil, vegetation, wildlife, moisture, the amount and type of use the area receives, and the overall effect of their own use—and then use their judgment to determine which practices to apply.

Perhaps this caring approach is best expressed in the beliefs of an old Eskimo man, related by the Arctic explorer Knud Rasmussen. "His philosophy of life," wrote Rasmussen, "was to the effect that we human beings know so very little of life and its controlling forces that we have an imperative duty, not only to ourselves but also to those we hold dear, to live as carefully as possible . . ."

The practices found in the following pages describe ways of caring for wildlands. But even more important, they point to that larger relationship that is the inevitable goal of any land ethic. By accepting responsibility for our remaining wildlands, we may yet learn to care about all earth's landscapes.

Grey Wolf

Will Waterman

Chapter
Two

◆

Backcountry Travel

◆

Examine the gear of someone who is about to embark on a backcountry journey, and you'll most likely find an organized pile of lightweight equipment—everything from trimmed map borders to shortened toothbrush handles. Why such fastidious organization? The answer lies less in the equipment than in a desire for careful preparation. What do I absolutely need, and what can I leave behind?

These days, thoughtful backcountry visitors are asking another question: How can I travel through wildlands so that I leave as little impact as possible? Many are learning that the same care and planning that contribute to a successful journey also serve to minimize disturbance to other visitors and the environment.

Methods of wildland travel vary greatly, but with few exceptions, mechanized recreation is either prohibited or impossible (or both). Hiking, horses, rafts, and canoes or kayaks remain the primary modes of transportation for most visitors. Although many of the recommendations we suggest apply to all methods, we look primarily at how to reduce the impact of the most frequent means of backcountry travel—hiking.

The Impact of Hiking

A superficial look at the numbers raises doubts about whether there really is an impact problem caused by backcountry travelers. Even though wilderness areas receive millions of visitors each year, use intensity averages only about 0.5 visitor-days per acre—not much compared with other kinds of land use. Yet according to Washburne and Cole's survey of managers, crowding was a problem in over half of all wilderness areas. Why are so many managers complaining of crowding if visitor use is so low?

Visitors seldom distribute themselves evenly throughout a wilderness area. In fact, most users concentrate their activities on just 10 percent of the more than 80 million acres of designated wilderness. With this in mind, it's easy to see why managers are concerned about crowding and its effect.

Even more revealing is why so few acres are favored. The popular spots are often close to population centers—areas with easy access, scenic views, or attractions such as good fishing or pleasant camping. Researchers investigating individual wilderness areas have learned that people generally prefer to go where others have traveled; most often this means a trail.

In one study, Forest Service researcher Bob Lucas found that certain trails were more popular than others. In most cases, 20 percent of trail miles accounted for 60 to 80 percent of all use. Why do people concentrate on trails? Sometimes travel off established trails is prohibited or impractical, perhaps even dangerous; sometimes visitors just like the familiarity of human-constructed paths. Whatever the explanation, we users are profoundly affecting the areas we like the most—trails have become a small but crucial part of our backcountry.

But trails are declining in number. In the 1930s our national forests had 132,000 miles of trails; today there are fewer than 100,000 miles. The reasons for the decline are many. The primary reason, however, is that land managers deemphasized trails when fire control and timber harvesting became increasingly mechanized. As a result, road mileage increased while the number of trails de-

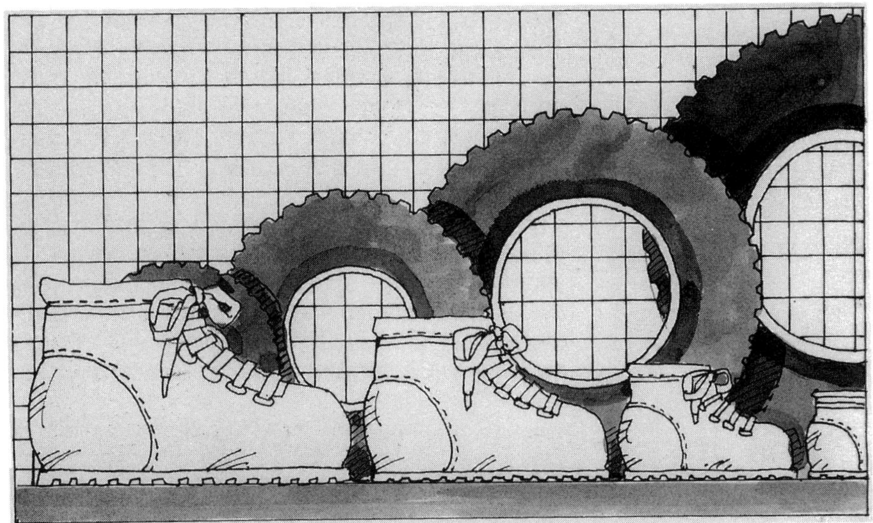

Bill Petersen

Road mileage in National Forests has increased as trail miles have declined, yet trail use has grown six-fold since 1960.

clined. Today, although our national forest backcountry has 25 percent fewer trails, the public's use of trails has steadily grown. For every person hiking a trail in 1960, six more people now leave their boot prints.

Increased trail use has prompted over half of all wilderness managers to list human-caused soil erosion and injury to vegetation as major factors in trail damage. The next most widespread trail problem is erosion caused by horses, mules, burros, and other packstock. Although only 11 percent of all parties entering the wilderness use pack animals, packstock damage on or near trails is considered a problem in almost half our wilderness areas.

Today, new trails are mostly wishful thinking, and existing trail maintenance budgets have been cut back severely. Some land managers have recommended increased off-trail use in the belief that visitor impact will spread more evenly throughout the backcountry, resulting in less damage to established trails. But cross-country travel has proven no panacea, say its opponents; indeed, the worst nightmare for these managers is a backcountry that looks in its entirety like their most heavily

eroded trail. They point to how thoughtless off-trail use in New Hampshire's White Mountains resulted in limiting travel strictly to trails. By 1977, surrounding alpine vegetation had suffered so much from cross-country use that scree walls were needed on both sides of a path to keep hikers confined to the trail.

As a user, you're often faced with a choice: Should you travel off-trail or on-trail? Our answer is that either can be appropriate, depending on your evaluation of the land and your skill in minimum-impact techniques. Although heavy use of existing trails does increase contact with other visitors and invariably leads to some environmental damage, trails fill an important niche in reducing impact in fragile off-trail areas. When trails are designed to accommodate use, disturbance of wildlife, soil, and vegetation is minimal. Off-trail plants and animals can find the solitude that is so critical to the preservation of entire ecosystems. Consequently, trails are often the best choice.

But there are times when cross-country travel is appropriate. Highly skilled travelers can often minimize their impact by choosing an off-trail route. The message seems clear: The user must carefully consider the trade-off when deciding to travel either by trail or cross-country.

When Traveling on Trails

Although most people prefer to travel on traditional, well-established trails, these trails can suffer abuse. Problems come when they receive too much traffic, or when hikers walk outside the path. Properly designed and maintained trails rarely suffer if visitors simply stay on them. But not all trails are well designed or properly maintained. What exactly happens when they deteriorate, and how can we minimize the damage?

The major environmental problems with trails are erosion, muddy stretches, and the development of informal trails. Most often, erosion and muddiness are effectively controlled by careful location and frequent maintenance. Still, there are several things visitors can do to avoid contributing to further damage.

When following existing trails, walk single file and stay on the path. Walking outside the tread—for example, traveling abreast or trying to avoid rocks or mud—breaks down the trail edge and widens the path. Such behavior also leads to the development of multiple trails, which scar some of our most beautiful meadows. Staying on the trail is sometimes difficult when trails are wet, yet this is when they are the most susceptible. Wearing a pair of well-fitted gaiters allows the hiker to walk briefly through wet or muddy areas with little discomfort.

David Cole

◀ *When hikers don't stay within the confines of a trail, multiple trails result.*

▲ *Hiking on the outside of a muddy trail breaks down the edge and widens the path. Here, the first and last hiker demonstrate the correct method.*

As with muddy stretches, it's better to cross low-angled snowbanks than to skirt them and thus create additional trails. If you're familiar with the area and know where the trail is under the snow, tramp a path to lead the way for others. When crossing high-angled snowbanks, however, safety is often the foremost concern; in this case, there may be no alternative to skirting the snowbank. Here it's better to risk widening the path by walking on the edge of the trail than to encourage the development of an entirely new impromptu trail. Sometimes merely avoiding popular backcountry areas during wet periods such as the spring thaw is the best practice.

Trails are usually designed to limit erosion and are often constructed with a low gradient of frequent switchbacks. Most hikers are tempted at times to shorten this distance. Yet shortcutting switchbacks causes erosion and damage to vegetation; it's perhaps the most common trail abuse. If the slope is vegetated, just a few plants are damaged at first. If the plants die, their roots no longer bind the soil, and soon the topsoil begins to wash away. Without topsoil, other plants can't recolonize the site, and runoff and erosion accelerate. Eventually, the shortcut becomes impassable, stripping away the corner of the switchback. Once erosion begins, it's increasingly difficult for nature to repair it. At high altitudes where growth is slow, it may never heal. Where shortcuts occur, you can help by throwing brush or logs across the shortcut, blocking hiker access. If an established switchback is impassable because of erosion or mud, walk on hard surfaces (such as rock, sand, or snow) as much as possible, and notify the managers responsible for that area. You may be surprised what action a few voices of concern can bring.

David Cole

Shortcutting trail switchbacks accelerates erosion, resulting in a scar almost impossible to heal.

The other major trail impact by hikers results from encountering other visitors, which means less solitude for both your group and the other party. The impact of this unavoidable situation can be lessened if you follow a few simple techniques. When taking a break, move some distance off the trail to a durable stopping place, preferably out of view of the trail. (Durable stopping places include rock outcrops, sand, other nonvegetated places, and sites with resistant vegetation, such as dry grassy meadows.) Here you can enjoy more natural surroundings, and other parties can pass by without contact. If you meet other hikers on a trail, move off to the side and stop; continuing to walk at the edge widens the trail. When you meet a horse party, allow it plenty of room, as horses frighten easily. Your entire group should move off to the same side of the trail, preferably the downhill side, and stand quietly until the horses pass. It's

Jim Allen

always easier for the wrangler to control a spooky horse if it bolts uphill rather than downhill. Sometimes it helps if one of your party talks in a low voice to the first rider, giving the horses advance notice of your presence.

When meeting a horse party, move off the trail and stand quietly until the horses pass.

When Traveling Cross-Country

Although not for everyone, cross-country travel opens up the other 90 percent of wildland few visitors see from trails. Many people assume that traveling off-trail is difficult. This is often true, but more important, cross-country travel is not for those who are unable to leave minimal traces of their passage—particularly those who hike in large groups, choose routes over fragile ground, or travel with packstock. For when you travel off-trail in

Will Waterman

For traveling cross-country, hike in groups of four to six people and spread out instead of following a single path.

remote backcountry, you must accept a special responsibility for the greater impact you may create.

Often the easiest cross-country practices are what *not* to do. Don't blaze trees, build cairns, or leave messages for members of your group in the dirt or sand. Such markers detract from other visitors' sense of discovery.

When traveling off-trail, select a route that avoids fragile areas, and spend as much time as possible on durable surfaces such as bare rock, sand and gravel, snow and ice, and other nonvegetated surfaces. Travel in small groups of no more than four to six people, and when not on a hardened surface, spread out rather than follow the same route.

Why all this concern for avoiding plants or unstable soil and minimizing the trampling any one place receives? Most plants soon die if stepped on more than a few times, and unstable soils start eroding even with light trampling. Once these processes begin, the impact quickly accelerates. An obvious path soon attracts others; footsteps on top of yours kill more plants and displace more soil. Trails develop where they are not wanted. Without careful route selection and maintenance of constructed trails, informal trails erode into permanent trenches that continue to deteriorate even without use. When these trails finally become too difficult to use, cross-country hikers move away, initiating trails elsewhere.

Studies show that for many types of vegetation, as few as fifteen people per year walking along the same route leave a discernible path. Even where effects aren't immediately obvious, trampling alters plant communities, changing them in subtle ways. Damage begins with injury to plant tissues; through loss of leaves or stems, plants lose their ability to photosynthesize food. Growth slows, resulting in smaller plants, fewer flowers, and reduced reproduction. Plants that are most susceptible to damage become less common, and once trampling reaches levels where all plants are affected, barren areas develop.

On steep terrain, it's less damaging to walk on rock or snow, following the most gentle slopes. On soil-covered surfaces, it's better to ascend than to descend, because boot heels carry extra force when moving downhill, increasing erosion. If slopes are so steep that it's necessary to dig toes and heels deeply into the surface to get a grip, some other route should be taken, if possible. Spreading out on steep slopes also reduces damage. When descending loose scree, move slowly and cautiously. Rapid descents can be fun, but they move sizable quantities of scree downhill, causing erosion that otherwise may take years to occur naturally.

Many of us know of places that were once little-known destinations but today are reached by webs of informal trails—the all-too-frequent result of cross-country travelers' not treating pristine areas with the care they require. Shun places where user-created trails are developing, and stay off trails that managers have closed. Avoid areas that are delicate, such as wet soils, or steep and unstable slopes. Where places are so fragile that even the passage of one person leaves a trail, it's better to walk single file so that only one trail is created. Although this may be the best you can do under the circumstances, challenge yourself in the future to find a route that avoids such impact.

Respecting Wildlife

When traveling through the backcountry, you're entering the homes of a myriad of animal types, from soil invertebrates to frogs, birds, deer, and bears. Although potential impact on each of these animals varies, the principle remains the same: respect their needs and minimize the disruption of their lives. (It seems difficult to apply this principle to mosquitoes when more than an occasional impact may be necessary.)

For most visitors, the simplest kind of wildlife disturbance to avoid is that which attracts animals, causing them to lose their wildness. When Ron Rau, an Alaska biologist, reports that wolves chase pickup trucks because oil pipeline workers toss sandwiches out of windows, it's easy to criticize such behavior. Backcountry visitors, however, are often equally at fault. When a bear ransacks a camp because someone carelessly left food lying about, the effects of wildlife disturbance hit home.

Although attracting animals is the most obvious problem, it's sometimes difficult to perceive other effects of our actions on wildlife. Few of us realize how camping near a water hole in the desert causes bighorn sheep to move to less productive habitat, and thus to decrease in number. We also alter the habitat of smaller animals when we disturb vegetation, dead or alive. Many small mammals and birds live in shrubbery, standing snags, and downed wood that are affected when campsites are trampled or firewood is gathered.

Another type of disturbance, especially of larger birds and mammals, is unintentional. Harassment occurs when you meet an animal on the trail, camp close to a water hole or a nest, approach animals to take a photograph, and in other seemingly innocuous ways. The animals' reaction is often excitement, alarm, and even flight, all of which consume energy needed for growth and reproduction. Obviously, animals that are healthy and have plenty of food and places in which to escape are more capable of withstanding disturbance than those that are underfed, highly parasitized, weakened by severe weather, or nesting or giving birth.

Shrubby Cinquefoil

Some animals are alarmed by unfamiliar types of disturbance; quick movements and loud noises are particularly stressful. Other animals are upset by stimuli reminiscent of predators, or when their escape routes are blocked. For example, a person suddenly appearing over a ridge will cause bighorn sheep to flee, yet humans approaching from below are often watched with little concern.

Sometimes rapid escape is harmful. Flight of pregnant animals has caused abortion. Frightened adults may run away and leave their offspring to die. There have even been accounts of disoriented mammals, such as deer and elk, drowning in escape attempts. More subtle consequences of flight have also been documented, such as frequently disturbed feeding areas that are abandoned for less productive ranges. In East Africa, harassment by well-meaning tourists following cheetahs on their daily hunts is forcing these diurnal predators to compete with nocturnal hunters for an ecological niche for which they are ill-suited. Crowding more and more animals on the ever-smaller undisturbed parts of our wildlands causes populations to become less healthy and dwindle in size. The upshot will be less wildlife, one of the most valuable qualities of our wildland heritage.

What can you do? First, learn about the animals indigenous to the place you're visiting. Your appreciation of the area and your chance of seeing wildlife will increase, and your knowledge will alert you to the times of year (particularly birthing seasons) and places (nest sites, watering and feeding grounds) where disturbance is most critical. Armed with this knowledge, you can make informed decisions about where to travel and camp. For example, observing animals from behind cover and at a distance, and collecting water from a spring but camping out of sight are simple means of avoiding disturbance.

Wildlife should be enjoyed, but remember that you're entering the animals' home. With knowledge, respect, and a lot of care, you can avoid adversely affecting them. As always, the need for care increases as you explore increasingly remote off-trail areas. These areas are the last bastions for truly wild species; they have no place else to go.

Keep in Mind

Most backcountry visitors prefer not to encounter other people. In a study of visitors in four wilderness areas, Forest Service researcher George Stankey discovered that three out of four visitors preferred having no contact with other backpackers.

A number of simple things will minimize contact with other parties. Whenever possible, visit the backcountry during seasons or days of the week when use is low. Avoid travel when the environment is particularly fragile, however, or when animals are susceptible to disturbance.

Travel in small groups. Although large parties usually represent only a small percentage of total use, they have a disproportionate impact on the experience of others they encounter when traveling the backcountry. In Stankey's study, most users preferred contacts with small rather than large groups. Given the choice between meeting one large party per day or ten small parties, most people preferred the smaller parties.

What is the optimum group size? Researchers admit that any "optimum" is arbitrary; still, most regard parties of more than ten or twelve individuals as large. Even if you're part of a large group, you can reduce your impact by hiking and camping in groups of no more than four to six people. Four is a commendable goal, especially for cross-country travel, because in case of sickness or injury, one person can stay with the victim while two people go for help. A group of four is also small enough to minimize impact on other visitors, the environment, and wildlife—especially bears—when traveling off-trail.

Whatever the time of year or the size of the group, whether on-trail or off-trail, always travel quietly. All senses are heightened in the silent, slow pace found in wildlands. Such a setting is conducive to understanding more about the subtle rhythms and balances of nature. If you travel quietly, you will be more aware of your environment, wildlife will be less disturbed, and other visitors will appreciate the solitude.

Columbine

Brightly colored clothes and equipment have limited advantages in the backcountry, despite their attractive appearance in store windows. To minimize the likelihood that others will see you and your camp, wear and carry earth-colored clothes and equipment, particularly tents. Although vivid yellows, oranges, and purples may be the hues of an alpine hillside in summer or autumn, bright human colors reinforce the feeling of crowdedness. (An exception is any small object, such as a tent peg or handkerchief, that poses the hazard of being left behind if its color is muted; these smaller objects cannot be seen from a distance.) Many backcountry users argue that manufacturers set the present trend toward bright colors, but a conscientious buying public has been known to alter fashion in the past.

Always choose a hiking boot or shoe with comfortable, yet safe, support. Too often, inexperienced hikers select a heavy, stiff-soled boot beyond the requirements necessary for the backcountry they plan to travel. One hiker, William Harlow, experimented with the amount of earth that was raised and exposed to erosion when a cleated hiking sole was pressed into wet soil. Harlow's experiment suggests that one hiker traveling one mile can leave 120 pounds of raised earth in his boot prints—earth that is ready to wash away with the first heavy rain. Although this is probably a worst-case example, it illustrates the potential damage of a lug-soled boot.

When hiking gentle country, consider using a

light pair of footwear. Grandma Gatewood, the 67-year-old woman who hiked all 2,000 miles of the Appalachian Trail three times, wore a pair of sneakers. Although such light shoes are not appropriate for heavy packs or boulder and snow fields in the Cascades or the Rockies, consider slipping into a pair of lightweight shoes once a campsite is selected.

Carry out all of your litter and any that was left by others. On the way out—when your pack is light—try to pick up a little extra. Some hikers even reserve an empty pack pocket for trash found on the trail. Allow others a sense of discovery by leaving rocks, plants, and other objects of interest as you found them. Enjoy an occasional edible plant, but don't deplete the surrounding vegetation or disturb plants that are either rare or do not reproduce in abundance (such as morel mushrooms and many edible lilies).

Traveling with dogs is prohibited in most national parks and increasingly discouraged in many other backcountry areas. A growing number of managers and users alike feel that a pet's place is in the home, not in our remaining wildlands. Arguments against dogs in the backcountry center around the tendency of unrestrained dogs to chase wildlife, defecate in or near water sources, and generally harass other users. In wildlands where coyotes or wolves are found, another argument has recently surfaced: the tracks of a dog rob others of the certain knowledge that similar tracks may belong to resident wildlife. Yet many visitors feel that dogs have a place in the backcountry, especially if the owner accepts the special responsibility of minimizing the problems a dog may cause. One way to control a dog in the backcountry is to leash it or load it with a pack. A pack keeps the dog close and restrains it from chasing wildlife, particularly if the pack is kept heavy enough. Like a carelessly constructed fire, dogs can have adverse effects and are certainly not necessary to the enjoyment of a backcountry experience. Still, when restrained, they are a comfort to many users and need not be a problem.

Finally, whether you travel by trail or cross-country, always assume someone will be passing in your footsteps. Strive to make your presence invisible to them. We aren't alone in our wildlands, and even though our impact may seem small, the overall effect of our presence in the wilderness is cumulative.

Your camps, after all, are the spots in the wilderness of which you have special knowledge; it is your campsites that you particularly remember.
—John Hart,
from *Walking Softly in the Wilderness*

Joel Rogers

Chapter

Three

Selecting and Using a Campsite

An experienced leader in the backcountry often shows puzzling behavior as the day draws to a close. Campsite after campsite, all of which are acceptable to other members of the group, may be passed up. Perhaps this tenting area may not be the flattest, the tired and disgruntled say, but rearrangement of a few boulders will make it comfortable. Or if the nearest spring lies just beyond a muddy trail through a wet meadow, they offer to make a new path. What kind of perfect campsite is this leader looking for, anyway?

"Perfect" may not be the proper term, since seldom does a site have the ideal qualities from everyone's perspective. Yet certain characteristics are generally agreed upon: level spots for tents, with ample room for camp chores; water nearby for washing and cooking; deadwood, if you plan to have a campfire; protection from weather; a beautiful view; and last, but not least, seclusion from campers outside your group. How does one arrange each camp to provide all of these qualities? One doesn't. As author John Hart says, "The perfect camp is found, not made."

The more one travels in the backcountry, the more one is on the lookout for naturally comfortable, isolated campsites—those with the fewest

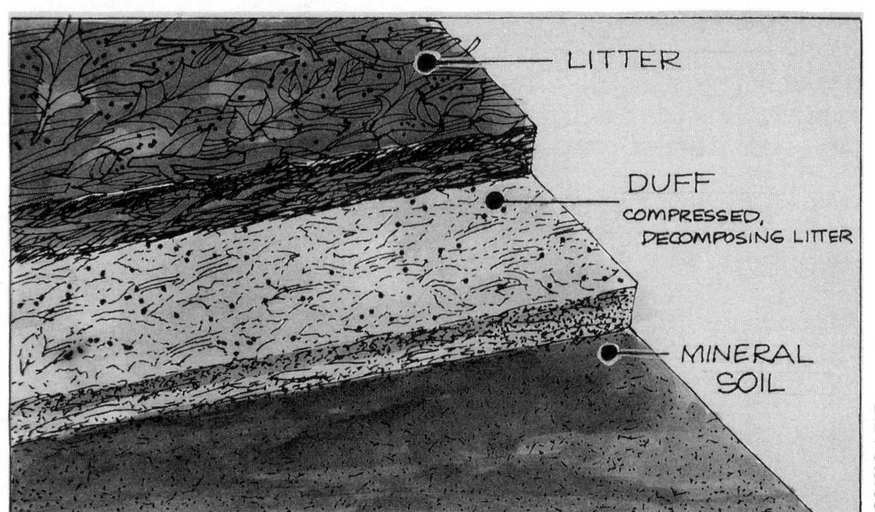

The organic layers of soil (duff and litter) disintegrate under increased trampling, exposing bare mineral soil, which quickly erodes.

alterations necessary. If it's true that your campsites are what you remember most about a wildland journey, then a night spent sliding down a steep slope, worrying about a leaning tree above your tent, or listening to a noisy group nearby is not soon forgotten. As your experience grows, you begin to watch for good campsites throughout your traveling day, even stopping early if you come across one that has exceptional attributes.

Today, simply finding an isolated and comfortable campsite is not enough. The site should be durable as well—durable from both an environmental and a social aspect. You must choose a campsite that will be the least damaged by your stay, and you must not harm the wilderness experience of others.

When Campsites Suffer

Social impact is particularly pronounced at campsites. Several studies have found that wilderness visitors are much more sensitive to meeting other groups in camp than to meeting them on the trail; campsite solitude is extremely important. Yet campsite environmental impacts are both serious and widespread. In Washburne and Cole's study of wilderness managers, more than 70 percent listed vegetation loss and soil compaction at campsites as frequent problems.

Sandhill Crane

At first, the effects of camping seem insignificant. Most visitors hardly notice them—some minor trampling of vegetation, blackening of a few rocks used to build a fire ring, or a little less firewood close to camp. With more use, however, it gets worse. Vegetation disappears from large portions of the campsite, and plants that survive are different from those growing just beyond camp. Under increased trampling stress, the organic layers of soil—surface litter, such as leaves, twigs, and needles, and subsurface duff, or decomposing litter—disintegrate and erode, exposing bare mineral soil. This soil increasingly compacts with additional trampling, restricting the movement of air and water to plant roots. As less water percolates into the soil, surface runoff increases. The runoff, in turn, increases erosion and makes the campsite even larger.

Impact can reach alarming levels. In the Eagle Cap Wilderness in Oregon, David Cole found that more than 90 percent of the ground vegetation in campsites had been destroyed by trampling. In addition, 95 percent of the trees had been damaged by people collecting firewood, tethering horses, or hacking trees with axes. What was particularly disturbing was that more than one-third of the trees had actually been cut down. Such campsites are forested by the "living dead"; they will remain forested only until the present generation of trees dies.

Compared with nearby undisturbed sites in the Eagle Cap, soil compaction and erosion were prominent; roots were exposed on more than one-third of the remaining trees. The size of campsites was large, many sites had multiple fire rings, and some sites had actually joined each other to form huge disturbed areas.

Campsites can rapidly deteriorate to this point. Investigating newly opened campsites in the

Boundary Waters Canoe Area in Minnesota, Lawrence Merriam and his associates at the University of Minnesota discovered that most site damage occurred in the first few years after the site opened. Once deterioration occurred, Merriam concluded, recovery took a long time; little improvement was expected in even ten or fifteen years. In similarly disturbed alpine areas in Colorado, recovery may take as long as 1,000 years.

But why are some campsites more seriously damaged than others? Researchers conclude that three major factors influence how much change occurs on a site: the amount of use the site receives, the behavior of its users, and the location of the campsite itself.

Amount of Use

Common sense dictates that of all factors, the amount of use a campsite receives is the most important; the more people using the site, the greater the impact. Actually, this is only partly true. Many frequently used sites are in much better condition than some sites used infrequently. Although almost all campsites sustain noticeable damage when camped on more than one or two nights every year, after a certain amount of camping, further use doesn't have much added effect. Studies in the subalpine forests of both Oregon and Montana show that additional use of sites that are already used approximately ten nights per year is unlikely to lead to further deterioration.

These results suggest two choices for minimizing damage. First, in order to keep impact as small as possible, we can spread ourselves so widely that no campsite is used more than one or two nights per year. Alternatively, we can camp over and over again on the same few sites, recognizing that these places will be significantly impacted, but that our impact will be confined to a very small part of the backcountry. A third option—camping on moderately impacted sites—is not realistic, because such sites are vulnerable to rapid deterioration with only minor increases in use.

An investigation of two popular lakes within the Eagle Cap Wilderness confirms this last point. More than 200 campsites were found within half a square mile; conspicuous evidence of impact was almost everywhere. Yet deterioration could have been confined to a few frequently used campsites, leaving the surrounding land in a relatively pristine condition. What began a few years ago as moderate or low impact of many different campsites quickly grew into one large scar on the land.

Trumpeter Swans

Type of Use

Frequently used campsites are affected far more by what you do when you're there than by how many times you're there. Campsites used by horse parties are often in worse condition than backpacker sites. In the Spanish Peaks Primitive Area in Montana, for example, researcher Sidney Frissell found horse camps to be ten times larger than hiker camps, with seven times as much bare ground.

Although hiking parties of fewer than five persons are nearly three times as common as larger parties, the effect of party size on campsites has never been formally studied. Obviously, a large group affects an undisturbed site more rapidly than a small one because trampling is that much greater. A large party also affects a larger area because of its need to spread out. On established campsites, however, a greater number of people in a group needn't contribute to unusually severe disturbance, as long as they confine their activities within the boundaries of the existing site.

Campsite Location

Of the three factors that affect campsites, location may be the most critical. Most people like to camp by lakes and streams. One study in Montana by Perry Brown and John Schomaker suggests that lakes may be the single most important factor in campsite selection. Ninety percent of all campsites had views of a lake, while only 6 percent lacked a view of any water. Such findings explain why campsites in the worst condition are often found at the edge of water.

Meadows are also favorite locations, and until a few years ago, visitors were admonished to always avoid choosing them as campsites. Yet recently, researchers have found sites in some meadows to be less altered than those in forests. In the Bob Marshall Wilderness in Montana, David Cole learned that campsites in grasslands and open forests with a grassy understory lost less than half as much vegetation as campsites located in dense forests. What does this mean if you're looking for a durable campsite? Although wet meadows are fragile and subject to human disturbance, dry meadows are less so—especially dry meadows with grass as the dominant vegetation. From strictly an environmental-impact viewpoint, a forest with any kind of ground vegetation other than grass is a poor choice for a campsite.

The Land Manager's Response

From this brief look at the effects of camping, it is obvious that the choice of a campsite is more complex than just finding an isolated and comfortable place to spend the night. To complicate the picture, sometimes the choice of where to camp isn't left up to the visitor at all, especially in areas that are the most crowded. For instance, land managers often discourage camping near all water sources. In fact, fully 30 percent of wilderness areas prohibit camping within a specified distance of all lakes and streams (usually a 200-foot setback), and many observers believe it won't be long before we see this regulation in almost all backcountry lands.

Another type of restriction limits users to specific campsites. In this "sacrifice site" concept, a few areas are sacrificed so that the rest remain undisturbed. Most damage occurs with dispersed use, some managers argue, and if everyone camps wherever they want, a greater proliferation of impacted camping sites will be the end result.

What's the alternative if you don't wish to be told where to camp? There isn't one in those areas where past visitors have acted irresponsibly and impact is severe. These places are too damaged to allow even careful users the possibility of creating additional impact; camping in specified sites or a suitable distance from water is the only reasonable solution. In such cases, we can only hope land managers are judicious in restricting specific highly impacted campsites and do not blanket the entire area with a single harsh rule. For the vast majority of our remaining pristine or moderately impacted backcountry lands where unregulated camping still predominates, users must take responsibility before their impact makes restrictions common fare.

Making the Choice

Selecting an appropriate campsite is probably the most difficult and most critical aspect of minimum-impact backcountry use. The choice requires the greatest use of judgment and information, involving trade-offs between environmental and social impacts.

Where to camp should be based on the intensity and type of recreational use in the area, the fragility of vegetation and soil, the likelihood of disturbance of wildlife and other visitors, an assessment of previous impacts, and your party's potential to cause impact. All of these criteria must be evaluated if you wish to avoid causing irreparable damage to a campsite.

Where to begin? First, choose a campsite that won't be damaged by your stay; it must be durable and reasonably distant from other campers. The point made previously bears repeating: research suggests that you'll cause the least damage when you camp on pristine sites that are durable and show no sign of previous use, or on popular high-impact sites so heavily damaged that further use will cause little additional deterioration. Low- or moderate-impact sites (those that show obvious signs of prior use but with a substantial amount of vegetation still surviving) should be avoided. Such sites deteriorate rapidly with further use; if unused, however, they eventually recover. Refer to the photos if you have any doubt about what a pristine, low-impact, or high-impact site looks like.

Joel Rogers

Although this high-impact campsite shows severe damage, it's better to camp in such places in popular areas rather than create additional campsites.

How to Select and Use a High-Impact Site

High-impact sites are popular locations where most of the ground vegetation has been lost due to trampling. Where should you camp if you find yourself in such an area? Although the temptation may be strong to select a pristine or low-impact campsite, don't! It is always better to choose a high-impact site in frequently visited areas than to risk creating yet another campsite.

When selecting a high-impact site, look for one in a concealed, forested location with comparatively little ground vegetation, preferably in thick forest litter and duff. If mineral soil exposure is kept to a minimum, soil compaction and erosion will also be reduced.

If a site with thick duff isn't present, try to find one that naturally lacks vegetation and duff—one on bedrock, gravel, or sand. If possible, avoid areas with obvious soil erosion or serious root exposure, as well as those that have coalesced into large campgrounds. In popular areas, however, these may be the only sites available.

Avoid high-impact sites in meadows and on the edges of forests. Social impact is severe in these places, and they are often critical wildlife habitat. Camp away from water sources, trails, other campers, and "beauty spots" such as lakes and streams. These choice campsites are often prime locations for other people's enjoyment of the area, so take extra time to seek a more secluded site.

When setting up camp, don't sprawl out. Choose a site large enough to accommodate your group without risking damage to the edge of the site; such damage always leads to site enlargement. Set up your tents and "kitchen" in places that have already been affected, with well-developed paths between tents and the cooking area. Be careful not to step on tree seedlings. Seedlings are extremely fragile, and many sites have few young trees to replace overstory trees when they die.

When leaving camp, make sure that it's clean and attractive and will appeal to the next group.

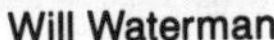

Will Waterman

David Cole

Remember—you want to encourage others to use your site, not damage a new one. On many high-impact sites, it is appropriate to clean up the site and dismantle excess fire rings, as well as constructed seats and tables. Properly located facilities such as a single fire ring, however, should be left alone; dismantling them only causes additional impact, for they will most likely be rebuilt.

Camping in high-impact areas often proves frustrating if you're an experienced camper. You may feel you are just contributing to the growing problem of abuse. The truth is, there's not a lot you can do to improve the site; it won't recover unless it is closed to all use. Still, there is much you can do to keep the damage from spreading. Be satisfied that you're helping to decrease the total number of damaged areas by camping on just a few selected sites, and by choosing ones that are the least visually obtrusive. You can encourage others to do the same by leaving the site as clean and appealing as possible.

◀ *The best pristine campsites are located on durable surfaces, such as dry grass, snow, or rock. They show no sign of previous use and probably will not be camped on more than one or two nights a year.*

▲ *This low- or moderate-impact campsite shows obvious signs of use, but a substantial amount of vegetation still survives. If the campfire ring is dismantled and the wood and rocks are scattered, it should eventually recover. With continued use, however, it will soon deteriorate into a high-impact site.*

How to Select a Pristine Site

Choosing a pristine campsite requires considerable skill and judgment. First, the site should be well away from popular areas. Second, it should show no sign of previous use or impact; either others haven't camped there before, or it has been so long that their impact is impossible to detect. (For clues, look for disturbed vegetation or charcoal from old campfires.) Finally, because evidence of your stay may tempt others to camp there, leave as few signs as possible. In short, camp on a durable surface.

Surfaces without vegetation or well-developed soils are ideal. Rock outcrops rate the best. Gravel bars, sandy beaches, snow, and ice periodically change or are removed by natural events—floods, tides, snowfall, and snowmelt—and they are also durable.

Surfaces with developed soils but no vegetation, although less desirable, are also durable. Your stay may cause minor soil compaction, but vegetation won't be disturbed, and recovery should be rapid. Be careful, however, not to damage a site with sparse vegetation. Scattered plants uproot more easily than those found in dense mats. This is particularly true of plants growing on a forest floor. Such plants are typically tall, leafy, and spreading (characteristics that help them capture the forest light) and crush easily. If you camp in a forest, choose a site with virtually no vegetation, or seek a more resistant alternative.

One type of vegetation that is always more durable than a vegetated forest floor is dry grass. Grasses grow in mats or tufts; their leaves and stems are often tough and densely clustered. Grass provides a cushioning effect, and its roots keep soil particles bound together. Thus, densely matted grass meadows, if they are dry, are always better choices than forests with sparse undergrowth. Camping in such meadows may have a visual impact on other visitors (and this should be considered), but the environmental effect of a night or two of camping on dry grass is likely to cause less damage than in the adjacent forest.

Plant structure determines the resistance of other types of vegetation. Some plants are woody; others are not. Broad-leaved nonwoody plants—from common wildflowers to rare orchids—don't survive trampling. Erect, succulent stems snap off underfoot, and broad leaves quickly shred. Woody plants seem resistant, but they, too, are often fragile, except in the case of a shrub or tree that's large enough to avoid being trampled. Once damaged, woody plants recover slowly, and new ones must usually grow from seed. Therefore, tree seedlings and low-growing shrubs are often the most susceptible to trampling.

The rule of thumb for pristine sites? Always try to find a nonvegetated campsite. If you have to choose between vegetated sites, look first for dense patches of dry grass and avoid vegetated forest floors and sites with low-growing shrubs as much as possible.

Golden-Mantled Ground Squirrel

How to Use a Pristine Site

On pristine sites, it's best to spread out tents and cooking areas, avoid using the same routes, and move camp every night if you suspect damage to plants or soil—practices exactly opposite from those of high-impact sites. Since repeated compression of soil and vegetation is the culprit in campsite deterioration, the objective is to minimize the number of times the site is trampled. Wear soft-soled shoes, such as running shoes, around camp. Minimize activity in your kitchen and places where packs are stashed, and watch where you walk to avoid crushing vegetation. Take alternate paths to water, and reduce the number of trips by carrying a large collapsible water container.

Both dispersal of activities and short stays are particularly important for large groups. When leaving, camouflage the area by covering any scuffed-up places with duff or other native materials. If you are camping in a grassy meadow, use your fingers or a fallen branch to rake the compressed areas where tents have flattened the grass. Remember: You are trying to camouflage your campsite so that no one will be likely to choose it again soon.

Keep in Mind

In any kind of campsite, pristine or high-impact, it almost goes without saying that you should leave the area as clean as you found it (and even cleaner if possible). Never dig trenches for tents or excavate shoulder or hip depressions, cut or break standing trees or branches, or pull up plants or embedded rocks to make a more pleasant camp. If you clear the sleeping area of surface rocks, twigs, or pine cones, replace these before leaving. Remember that young vegetation is easily damaged; in spring, camp on snow to avoid trampling plants early in their life cycle.

A backcountry camp always benefits from being well organized. If you have laundry to dry or equipment to air out, try to keep these items out of sight of other visitors, especially around lakeshores or open meadows. Always make sure your food is protected from animals.

Finally, stop early enough each day to choose an adequate camp. You must have sufficient time and energy to find a resistant site. Too often, tired travelers pulling in at the end of a long day on the trail shortchange themselves, the rest of us, and all our remaining wildlands by not taking the time to select a durable campsite. Ironically, these same travelers would never think of dropping even a piece of coconut out of their trail food.

Will you ever find that "perfect" campsite? Sure. They're sometimes few and far between, but they do exist. In the meantime, consider what you mean by "perfect." It may only mean that you take one last look as you pack for another day of travel, knowing that whoever comes upon your campsite will never imagine anyone had camped there the night before.

Wolverine

Will Waterman

Chapter

Four

Fires and Stoves

Humans are creatures of fire. Indeed, the realization that fire is controllable was a first step on the long journey from our past. Rule over fire soon became a symbol of not only survival but also the ability to effect change. Yet for how long did humankind regard starlight scattered across the night sky as distant campfires? Even when humans outgrew such simple thoughts, they still believed that the fire of stars spun about a universe with earth at its center.

Like glowing embers, some ideas die slowly. It wasn't until the beginning of the seventeenth century that Johannes Kepler demonstrated that earth was not the center of the universe, and that all the fires beyond did not orbit our planet. Now, as we move even further away from human-centered beliefs, we shake our heads as we realize how long our forebears stubbornly hung on to them. Yet even though we like to believe we are more sophisticated today, we're reluctant to lose our identity with fire itself. When we hike into the mountains or canoe a river, we move closer to our campfires as night falls. Campfires warm us, cook our food, or simply make us feel secure, stirring something deep within. They have a hold on us, refusing to burn out, even as they once held back the darkness of nights long ago.

How can anyone go camping without a fire? Ernest Thompson Seton, one of the first advocates of camp craft, insisted, "What is a camp without the evening campfire? It's nothing but a place in the woods where some people have some things."

Will Waterman

Carelessly constructed campfires are perhaps the single most common impact in the backcountry.

Yet today we see growing numbers of backcountry users rejecting fires in favor of lightweight stoves.

Although in some cases the lack of available firewood may have forced this change, the truth is that many users have made a free choice to use stoves. With the notable exception of national parks (over 40 percent prohibit campfires), few wildernesses ban campfires. It appears that an ethic practiced by conscientious users may yet overtake a regulation before it becomes the law of the land.

But if fires are so important to the camping tradition, why are people lighting up their stoves? The answer can be found in campsites from Mount Katahdin to Baja—carelessly constructed campfires leave a scar on the land, which makes them perhaps the single most common impact in the backcountry. Long after grass revegetates a trampled campsite and new trees take root in an eroded switchback, the blackened smudge of a campfire tells of human use. Campfire scars continue to burn deep into wild country, lending credence to what experienced users have long advocated: use of a stove is almost always preferable to building a campfire.

The Dark Side of Fires

In addition to the long-term effect of blackened fire rings, campfires often leave less obvious impacts. Fires demand fuel, and when those fires are built repeatedly in one area, surrounding trees—first, down and dead timber and finally, even living trees—show the abuse of wood-gathering. In high-impact areas, thoughtless campers often saw small trees a foot above the ground and strip standing trees of their twigs and lower branches. Once a tree falls, its limbs are removed, and the remainder of the trunk is axed or sawed along its length. Even soft, rotted wood is collected for the fire-building ritual, no matter how poorly it burns. Soon a campground has a "cleaned-out" look; all the wood is gone, and the repeated demand for campfires keeps it that way.

Besides not contributing to these impacts, stove users who have kicked the campfire habit profit from freedom and simplicity around the campsite. No time is spent gathering firewood, there is no fire ring to disguise, and finally, there is no isolation from a night world. Once the evening meal is cooked and the roar of the stove dies out, the sounds and sights of darkness return. No longer does the flickering light from a campfire divide the night into close and far, or keep a coyote or the Milky Way beyond ear or eye. Nighttime invades your campsite, your eyes gather their night vision, and you find yourself part of a larger world that would be obscured by any campfire.

What We Know

Certain consequences of campfire building have recently come to light. For instance, the impact of campfires increases with elevation. When forests of whitebark pine, mountain hemlock, and lodgepole pine are subjected to campfire use, whitebark pine—a common high-altitude western species—comes out on the low end. In fact, forests dominated by whitebark pine appear to be too low in productivity to sustain high levels of firewood collection (see Chapter Nine).

Consumption of firewood also varies with user activities. Visitors tend to build fires in proportion to the size of the fire ring; fires in small rings consume less wood than those in large rings. (An average fire ring is about twenty-five inches in diameter.) In addition, when searching for firewood, small groups normally don't go more than 200 feet from their campsite; larger groups travel greater distances, enlarging the impact on the collection area. These findings cast doubt on a common assumption among campers that cooking fires consume a significantly smaller amount of wood than "social" fires used for companionship.

In another study by Dennis Fenn and associates investigating the effect of fire on soil, researchers discovered that heat from a large campfire is capable of altering organic matter to a depth of four inches or more, with a 90 percent loss in the upper inch of soil. The resulting sterilization of the underlying soil may at first appear unimportant, but as firesites continue to multiply in high-impact areas, the opposite is true. In California's Yosemite National Park, over 300 fire rings have been reported at a single lake, many of them past scars that refuse to heal.

Are Campfires Taboo?

No, not by a long shot in most backcountry. Although much of the preliminary evidence against fires is incriminating, many otherwise conscientious users who practice minimum-impact techniques refuse to give them up. To these hikers, rafters, and canoeists, campfires are a powerful tradition and contribute much to the quality of a wildland experience. Stove converts tell redeeming tales of nighttime discoveries; campfire advocates affirm the qualities of a night held back by firelight. Listening to both sides, one concludes that no matter what further research may eventually reveal, campfires are here to stay.

Although stoves are usually preferable to campfires, there are times when fires are appropriate—if they are constructed with care. Most campfires, however, should be considered luxuries, not necessities, especially in areas of established or growing popularity. The final rule of thumb for campfire advocates might be better stated this way: bring a stove, and know when and where to use it.

American Avocet

Where Fires Are Acceptable

A wild river coursing through a pristine Alaska spruce forest, a high-impact campground in a lodgepole forest in Wyoming, a beach littered with driftwood along the Olympic Peninsula—all these locations may be appropriate sites for those visitors wishing to build campfires.

Generally, both an area that is infrequently visited and shows virtually no sign of former human use (pristine), and a popular area where use is concentrated (high-impact) are ideal settings for campfires. The important locations to avoid are low-impact campsites, since with any additional use these often rapidly deteriorate and develop into high-impact sites.

Besides the criteria used in campsite selection, appropriate campfires all have five necessary ingredients in common: they are safe, damage to the site is minimal, construction of the fire is simple, firewood is abundant, and cleanup and camouflaging of the site are easy.

Safety

During the past two decades, research has created a dilemma for land managers who once be-

believed that fire was the worst fate that could befall a forest. With the growing awareness that naturally occurring fires have long been a source of rejuvenation and disease control in forest ecosystems, managers have had to amend their stand against wildfire. After scores of years and millions of dollars spent admonishing the public about the evils of wildfire, Smokey the Bear has suddenly developed a stutter. Fire can be good after all.

Even though managers are making room in their management schemes for small, periodic, lightning-caused fire, fires started by human carelessness are still out of favor. The fact is that each summer, campfires escape control, burning large tracts of backcountry. Many of these tragedies could be avoided simply by using extra caution when constructing campfires. Who wants to be responsible for destroying an entire forest of mountain hemlock just because he or she did not take the time to properly construct a campfire?

As a first precaution, always build campfires far from dry grass, trees, branches, and root systems, and never leave a campfire unattended. Think about what an upslope or downslope wind might do to your fire and where those sparks might fly. Avoid building fires on windy days or during periods of drought. Finally, many areas have regulations restricting the use of campfires. Be sure you know and respect those regulations. They are often issued because massive forest fuel buildup, coupled with unpredictable winds, gives fire the potential to destroy entire backcountry areas.

Minimal Damage

If you have chosen a high-impact campsite in order to limit your impact but still wish to have a campfire, you should first ask yourself whether or not your use of available firewood will have further impact on the site. Provided there is abundant deadwood on the ground, your next decision is where to build the fire. In popular areas where high-impact sites are common, there is *no* excuse

Will Waterman

In popular areas with high-impact campsites, always construct campfires in an existing fire ring or where past fires have been built.

for building a fire where one has never been built before—your fire should always be constructed in an existing fire ring or in a place where past fires have been built. If you camp in a site that has numerous campfire scars, select one that is most pronounced and in the safest location.

Choosing a location on a pristine site requires more care. Even though firewood may be abundant, sloppily constructed campfires on undisturbed sites sterilize soil and damage vegetation, especially where trampling occurs at the fire's edge. You can minimize this impact, however, by choosing sites that are rocky or sandy, have exposed mineral soil, or are below the high waterline along watercourses. (See Chapters Seven and Eight for additional campfire practices.)

The best surfaces are bare mineral soil, thin duff (less than two to three inches thick), a flat rock, or as a last choice, very sparse vegetation. Never build a fire in duff more than four inches thick; the danger that the fire will spread is great in such organic soils. Avoid fires in any kind of vegetation—brush, grass, or young trees—unless it is so sparse that there is no chance you will damage plants by firesite construction or trampling.

Will Waterman

When building a pit fire in duff or litter, scrape or dig the pit several inches deep and make it larger than the area the fire will occupy.

Campfire Construction in Pristine Sites

Campfires should be built either on a mound of mineral soil or in a pit or hole dug into the ground. A decade ago, pit fires were all we at NOLS recommended. These fires were elaborate creations constructed in vegetated areas. Diligent care was taken to replace the original surface vegetation exactly as it had been removed. We even carried water to these sites in an effort to enhance their recovery. Investigation of these campfires after use, however, revealed not only damaged vegetation surrounding the site but also sunken depressions where the pits themselves had been dug. Moreover, as if to point out our error, animals had often excavated these old fire pits, even though no solid food had been deposited there. Regardless of the precautions we took, pit fires continued to live up to their inglorious name.

Our solution? We had the basic premise right, but the secret was to dig the pit in the correct location. Our practices soon evolved into building pit fires only in places with exposed mineral or sandy soil, avoiding vegetated areas.

Although construction of a pit fire in exposed mineral soil is possible in most areas, sometimes the only option is to dig a pit through duff and litter to mineral soil. After scraping away the thin duff and litter from the surface down to mineral soil, simply dig or scrape a shallow pit, several inches deep. Build your fire in this shallow pit. A wide pit will minimize the chance fire may spread into nearby duff and litter.

Although pit fires are usually the simplest low-impact fire to build in most backcountry areas, there are situations where you should avoid build-

Will Waterman

ing them at any time: directly under low limbs; in dry, thick duff; or where ground vegetation will most likely be damaged. In these places, a mound fire is a better choice.

Build the fire no larger than necessary to lessen the chance it may spread.

Mound fires are constructed of a layer of insulating mineral soil that is first removed, then spread over a flat rock, and finally returned to its original location after use. They are appropriate provided adequate mineral soil can be gathered without damaging the source area. Where can you find this mineral soil? Uprooted trees, sandy areas near streambeds, or exposed soil near rock or boulder areas where vegetation is not growing are all excellent sources.

To build a mound fire, choose an appropriate base—either a massive immobile rock, a portable rock, or even several small rocks fitted together to form a relatively flat surface. With a small hand shovel or trowel, gather mineral soil from a nearby source. If the distance to your fire site is far, carry the soil in a stuff sack or day pack turned inside out. Spread the soil at least three inches deep on top of the rock over an area greater than the fire will occupy. An expanded area is especially important; campfires always seem to grow larger than originally planned. (A mound that is twenty-four inches in diameter is usually sufficient for a small fire.) Then build your fire on top of this soil.

Will Waterman

Burn the coals down to ash, cooling the ash and surrounding soil with water if necessary. After the fire is completely out, scatter the remains far from the site.

Mound fires are a safe, effective alternative to pit fires if you make sure the rock base is always covered with an adequate layer of mineral soil. If you use a soil thickness less than three inches, you risk heating the underlying base, resulting in exfoliation of the rock as the crystals expand from the fire's heat. Never build a fire on a rock foundation without this protective layer. Besides splitting the rock or damaging attached lichens, at the very least this practice will cause a long-lasting carbon scar.

In backcountry areas where rocks are scarce, some users have resorted to carrying fire pans, a fireproof container or material upon which the fire is constructed. (Even a nylon sheet, covered with an adequate amount of soil, makes a good base.) Fire pans are increasingly common (and sometimes required) on popular river trips where extra weight is not a burden. (See Chapter Seven for a detailed description.) Finally, regardless of the construction, consider carrying a small grate if you plan to cook on a fire. Grates with metal legs prevent blackening of the rocks used for a base. They also keep pots from spilling, dousing firewood, and creating charcoal that otherwise would burn down to ash.

Firewood

Although availability of firewood is an important characteristic of an ideal campsite for many visitors, there is considerable disagreement over what constitutes an adequate supply. The best firewood is small in diameter (one or two inches thick) and found lying loose on the ground, *not* attached to

Will Waterman

down timber. Small pieces of wood are easier to burn to ash and are less critical to the ecosystem. If wood is not small and dry enough to break by hand, it won't burn completely and shouldn't be used. (Thus, you can leave your saw or axe at home.) Avoid using rotten wood. Although decaying wood usually makes for undesirable firewood, too often it has been utilized by fire users in high-impact campsites. Although little is known about firewood, a consensus is growing among researchers that decaying, rotting wood is critical to healthy forests.

Gather firewood away from your camp, and always leave some wood on the ground so the area doesn't look denuded. You can often minimize time and effort by walking 100 yards before collecting wood, rather than scrounging for the few pieces

Fill in the pit with the excavated soil and camouflage the site with duff and litter.

others might have left closer to camp. Collect only enough wood for a small fire; don't stockpile more than you plan to use. Finally, avoid burning food scraps and plastic. In a Sierra Club study headed by H. T. Harvey, incinerating leftover food required nearly 30 percent more wood than cooking it to begin with. Burning anything other than firewood makes combustion difficult, wastes wood, transfers large quantities of heat into the soil, and finally, makes cleanup difficult.

Will Waterman

A mound fire built on mineral soil spread over a rock base is an effective alternative to a pit fire.

Cleanup

Wise site selection and good campfire construction are meaningless without a thorough cleanup, for which you must allow sufficient time. Too often, a shabby job of cleaning a campfire site is related to how late you linger in your sleeping bag. Plan ahead, and don't be in a rush to leave camp. Even better, avoid a morning fire entirely by using your stove. If your campfire burned out completely the night before, the ashes will be cold, no water will be necessary to douse the fire, and cleanup will be minimized.

Regardless of whether you use a pristine site or an established fire ring, burn any remaining wood to ash at least thirty minutes before finishing with your fire. Heap larger, partially burned pieces of wood where the heat is greatest; add small pieces to keep the fire hot until only white ash remains. Crush any charcoal remnants. If you can sift your fingers through the ash and powder, your fire is out. Scatter these remains and any unburned firewood far from the site, and distribute them over a large area so that no sign of your fire will be noticeable.

When building your campfire in an existing ring on a high-impact site, only a moderate amount of cleanup is usually necessary. If multiple fire rings exist at your campsite, however, take extra time to dismantle them, leaving only your single, clean fire ring to attract the next user. (Always leave at least one fire ring in these sites; otherwise they'll most likely be built again, perhaps in a worse location.)

Will Waterman

Fires can be built on nearly any material if an insulating base of mineral soil is used.

Grind any leftover charcoal found in these other fire rings to powder, and scatter it away from the site; do the same with large quantities of ash. Any excess blackened rocks should be returned to their original locations, if possible, or scattered some distance from camp. Your cleanup will more than compensate for the effect of your fire on high-impact sites.

At a pristine site, scatter your fire's ash widely, and take pains to avoid discovery by others. If you constructed a mound fire, scatter the leftover ash and charcoal, then return the soil to where you originally found it; if the mound was built on a rock, rinse the rock off. When using a pit, fill it in with the excavated soil after dispersing the ash. Finally, disperse any excess firewood, and camouflage the site with mineral soil or litter—whatever matches the surroundings.

Will Waterman

Chapter
Five

Sanitation and Waste Disposal

It wasn't long ago that people discovered that uncleanliness shortened life. For centuries, humans left their refuse wherever it fell. Not until they became creatures of villages, towns, and finally cities did people make a connection between growing heaps of trash and human refuse, and plagues of cholera, yellow fever, and typhoid. In 2500 B.C. the Mahenjo-Doro of southern Asia established the first town drainage system for human sewage. Devising means of disposal of other waste products of civilization took a little longer. The Greeks built a municipal city dump in 500 B.C., and Rome even had a collection system to clean up after the gladiator games in the Coliseum. On especially festive days, some 5,000 bodies of gladiators, elephants, and tigers were carted to the pits at the edge of the city and left to rot.

Today, most of us who visit the backcountry return to life in the city. We live in a society that has identified the waste products of civilization as a source of human disease and has taken steps to remove them from our close association. Still, we are often uncomfortable talking about waste. As urban dwellers, we accept the modern-day mystery of waste management, complete with flush toilets, a municipal septic system euphemistically termed a "water-treatment facility," and a growling metal monster that comes through the alley and ingests last night's leftovers.

But where do these leftovers go? Most of us either don't know or don't want to know. For generations now, we have given the responsibility for what has always been an unpleasant task to someone else.

In a similar way, we have managed to carry the practice of avoiding responsibility for our waste into the backcountry. Until recently, we have discarded our refuse—from human body waste to pop-tops—as quickly and as far away from ourselves as possible. And we were thoughtless about it. If the Forest Service provided no garbage collection at a campsite, we dug a hole and buried our cans. If we found no outhouses, we chose the closest clump of trees and left our toilet paper to blow away in the wind. Once we traveled on, we didn't have to deal with the consequences of our waste.

Luckily today, although disposal of waste and trash is still a problem in some backcountry areas, we're cleaning up our act. Just as important, we've begun talking about it. "Pack it in, pack it out" is a popular saying now found on signs at nearly every trailhead. As longtime researcher Bob Lucas has observed, "Trash and litter in wilderness are much less common than twenty years ago, despite increased use."

But trash and litter are easy. What about those high-impact areas where human body waste is everywhere?

Sanitation

In their desire to change visitor behavior, backcountry managers have successfully utilized other popular sayings. "Take only photos, leave only footprints" is another well-known maxim. But by now you know that even footprints exact a heavy price from the land when too many fall in one place. Likewise, the hope of leaving only footprints when traveling on a backcountry journey ignores the simple fact that we humans regularly consume water and food and in return produce urine and feces. We have little choice but to leave our body waste as well.

Many visitors argue that body waste is part of a natural cycle, and if other animals disregard its deposition, so should we. In the case of urine, this is generally true; it is mostly a sterile waste product. Nevertheless, in developing countries where shistosomiasis is common, urine carries the infecting parasite. Urine also attracts wildlife, and these animals defoliate plants and dig up soil in their eagerness to ingest its salts. Urinating on rocks or in nonvegetated areas far from a water source is a simple solution to both of these problems.

Kingfisher

Solid waste is a different matter. The reason is that fecal waste is often the medium for disease; pathogens use feces to spread themselves and their offspring from one human to another. After the waste is deposited, the most common means of transmission are direct contact with feces, contact with a contaminated insect, or ingestion of contaminated water.

Water Pollution

In many wildland areas, water is a limited resource. Yet water is in demand for a variety of competing uses; it is necessary to plants and animals, and a focal point of most campsite activities. Life suffers when the quality of water declines, but those consequences are great when humans are the users. Once pathogens in sufficient quantity find a way into water, the risk of contamination increases dramatically.

How do backcountry areas measure up? The data are sketchy, but preliminary evidence indicates that most backcountry waters have surprisingly low levels of bacterial contamination. In one study, researchers led by Don Erman from the University of California at Berkeley investigated the water quality of Rae Lakes, one of the most popular lake basins in the Sierra Nevada. They found that bacterial levels in the water were usually low enough for safe drinking. A similar study examined water quality in a Montana watershed that had been closed to backcountry use. Researchers discovered that contamination actually decreased when the watershed was opened to visitors, presumably because wild animals—the principal contaminators—were scared away.

If you're starting to feel smug that the research backs up what you've always hoped was true whenever you took a sip from a mountain stream, don't. It is impossible to monitor the quality of every water source, and because animals other than man often contribute to bacterial counts, contamination can and does occur in some areas. Besides, bacteria represent only one kind of pathogen found in water. The most prudent recommendation still stands: Don't trust the quality of water in backcountry areas. Unfortunately, many users continue to ignore this advice.

In recent years, a new waterborne pathogen has reared its ugly head—a devastating intestinal protozoan named *Giardia lamblia*, that causes giardiasis. Although this disease is not usually fatal, some victims say that before you recover, you may wish it were. To term giardiasis "new" may not be precisely correct, for it's not clear whether contamination is spreading or whether it's merely being diagnosed more frequently. What is certain is that much of the surface water in even the most remote backcountry is severely contaminated with *Giardia*. In a study of pristine streams in the Sierra Nevada, Forest Service hydrologist Thomas Suk and his colleagues found that 35 percent of the water tested had dormant *Giardia* cysts. Exactly who are the culprits—humans, domestic cattle, or wild animals, such as beavers, ground squirrels, mice, and chipmunks—is uncertain and perhaps irrelevant as far as users are concerned. What is important is that Suk's research shows that this disease spreads through fecal contamination by both humans and other animals.

Thus, although most backcountry waters receive a passing grade on bacterial counts, many fail miserably because of this tiny microbe responsible for an extremely painful and debilitating form of dysentery. The warnings on backcountry signs are true; all users who don't sterilize their water are at risk, and sanitary precautions should be taken to minimize the further spread of giardiasis through human fecal contamination of water.

Lupine

The Choices

Even though most pathogens such as *Giardia* are spread through water, direct contact with feces or contaminated insects are also viable means of transport. Since any of these paths are possible, the best method of solid body waste disposal should ultimately serve three objectives: minimize the chance of water pollution, minimize the chance of anything or anyone finding the waste, and maximize the rate of decomposition.

For years, many established campsites in high-impact areas have been either blessed or cursed (depending on your point of view) with a traditional solution—outhouse toilets. Some users favor toilets as a necessary feature; others rebel at obtrusive structures in otherwise wild country. Research suggests that public opinion concerning toilets has shifted from positive to negative in the last two decades. Bob Lucas found that two-thirds of all visitors to the Desolation Wilderness in California opposed outhouses, despite heavy use of the area.

Considerable ingenuity has been devoted to developing alternatives to toilets in the backcountry. Some suggest the use of communal, user-created latrines; others advocate individual, shallow scrapings within a few inches of the soil surface, appropriately called catholes. Finally, there are those who simply recommend surface disposal.

Latrines have lost favor in recent years mostly because of their function: they concentrate human waste. If not properly sited, they have a high potential for water pollution, and are a possible source of insect contamination. Latrines also create a large area of disturbed soil, not only because of their initial excavation, but because of unavoidable trampling and compaction of nearby soil. In addition, latrines are frequently overfilled, making it difficult to cover them properly when they are finally closed. Like fire pits, latrines take a long time to decompose, giving animals time to find and dig them up, and to scatter the remains, thereby increasing the chance for human contact.

For these reasons, managers generally recommend individual catholes instead of latrines. The common belief is that soil microorganisms located in the organic layers close to the surface decompose feces in a short time, rendering them harmless. Researchers at Montana State University, led by Ken Temple, tested this theory by burying feces inoculated with pathogens underground for a year. Their results were disappointing. Substantial numbers of pathogens survived the entire year buried in the most organic part of the soil. Furthermore, numbers scarcely varied with either depth of burial or the type of site. Quite simply, the idea that shallow burial renders feces harmless in a short period is plainly wrong; buried feces can remain a health hazard for years.

Because both latrines and catholes present problems, some users advocate surface disposal. Decomposition is more rapid when feces are exposed to the sun and air than when buried. Unfortunately, surface disposal increases the likelihood of contact by humans or insects, and if improperly located, of water pollution as well.

The Best Choice

It seems clear that no means for the disposal of human waste in the backcountry—toilet, latrine, cathole, or surface disposal—is without problems. None can be unconditionally recommended for every situation. If toilets or latrines have been provided, use them. Otherwise, you must juggle the goals of minimizing water contamination and discovery by others with the goal of maximizing decomposition.

Where use is extremely low, the chance of discovery is small, and the distance from water is at

Will Waterman

Catholes are a popular backcountry way to bury human waste, but research shows that buried waste remains a hazard when decomposition is slow.

least 200 feet or more, no significant health hazard should result from surface disposal of your feces. Choose a dry, open exposure that's not likely to be visited by others. Scattering and smearing feces with a rock or stick maximize exposure to the sun and air.

In more popular places where most visitors hike, canoe, and camp, it's better to bury waste in catholes. Even though decomposition is slower than at the surface, it is more important to decrease the likelihood of contact with others. When traveling in a group, remember that the main objective is to disperse everyone's waste, *not* concentrate it. Choose a level spot, and dig a hole several inches deep in the organic layer of soil, where microorganisms are most abundant. When you're done, take a stick and mix soil with your feces for quicker decomposition. Then cover your cathole with at least

Will Waterman

Packaging food in plastic bags eliminates leftovers and potential littering of cans, bottles, or aluminum foil. After rationing, this NOLS Mount Denali expedition sent their leftover cardboard boxes out by dog sled.

an inch or two of topsoil. Finally, camouflage the surface.

Although latrines are the least desirable method, they may be necessary in areas where the number of disposal sites is severely limited. They may also be appropriate for long stays by large groups in popular areas. This is especially true of inexperienced campers who may be unable to carefully select a correct disposal site for a cathole. Dig the latrine when you first arrive in camp, and make sure everyone knows its location. A Sierra Club study of large camping groups found that selection of a latrine site was often given low priority by experienced group leaders; consequently, less knowledgeable members frequently placed the latrine too close to campsites or water sources.

If you have to dig a latrine, make it wider than it

is deep—but at least twelve inches in depth to minimize the chance that it will be excavated by animals or exposed by other people. After each use, cover the feces with soil and compress them by foot or with a shovel to encourage decomposition. Finally, always fill in the latrine once it gets within about four inches of the surface. (See Chapter Seven for a description of a portable latrine method.)

Clark's Nutcracker

Trash

In addition to natural by-products, we humans create additional waste. In the United States alone, each person produces a daily average of five pounds of garbage; over half a million tons of garbage are deposited across the country every day! With our growing mobility, it is inevitable that some of this effluent spills into the backcountry. In 1975, for instance, over twelve tons of trash and garbage were removed from Washington's Pasayten Wilderness using pack mules and helicopters; undoubtedly, much more was left behind.

Besides disposable food containers such as cans, bottles, and plastic, we're littering aluminum foil, toilet paper, tampons, and leftover food, just to mention some of the more commonly found items. Although a "clean camping" campaign has done much to raise the level of public consciousness in recent years, even the most experienced backcountry traveler is occasionally remiss. No matter how careful we are, it's extremely difficult not to lose an item or two when taking an extended journey. The trick in this case is to minimize the chance of loss.

The signs mean what they say: pack out whatever you pack in. To do this, however, be careful what you pack in. Most trash can be eliminated from the start with organized meal planning. Proportion and then package food in plastic bags instead of cans, bottles, or aluminum foil. Careful food preparation prevents most leftovers. If you have unavoidable surplus food, package it in plastic bags, and either eat it later or pack it out.

Scattering food, especially large amounts such as a burned pot of rice or noodles, attracts wildlife. Although scattering leftovers is unlikely to be serious in remote places, it's usually best to pack out what you can't (or won't) eat. Burial is ineffective because animals smell food and dig it up. Burning food, which is usually moist, requires an extremely hot fire. Often, your good intentions only result in a half-charred mess that smothers the fire and leaves unconsumed food, unburned charcoal, and a sloppy fire pit.

One exception to scattering leftover solid food is fish. Scatter the remains widely, out of sight of and away from campsites. Like moist food scraps, fish will not adequately burn unless your fire is exceptionally hot. In high-impact areas, people who fish should scatter fish leftovers far (at least 200 yards) from campsites. In alpine backcountry areas, don't throw these remains back into lakes and streams; the cool temperatures in mountain waters act like a refrigerator, preventing rapid decomposition. Fish remains that are slowly rotting on the bottom of crystal-clear lakes and streams provide a lasting reminder of careless humanity. (See Chapter Eleven for an exception to this practice in bear country.)

Burnables, and Those That Aren't

Today, traveling light for many visitors also means doing without that recent invention of civilization—toilet paper. Even though a growing number of users find simple satisfaction in pine cones, leaves, rocks, grass, or snow, others deem this too great a sacrifice. If you spend much time in popular backcountry areas, however, you'll understand why many say toilet paper has no place in wild country. Discarded, uncovered toilet paper remains long after feces disappear, and birds often carry it or wind blows it into nearby water sources.

If you use toilet paper, try to get by with a minimum amount. Be extremely cautious if you burn it: make sure the fire is out when you're done. More than a few forest fires have been started by carelessly burned toilet paper. (Consequently, some backcountry areas prohibit this practice entirely.) At the same time, make sure you leave no unburned pieces. Folded toilet paper is difficult to burn and, when covered with feces, won't burn at all. Unraveling the used sheets aids complete combustion. If fire danger is high or you have a difficult time burning the used paper, consider packaging it in a plastic bag until you can burn it later at a campfire. If campfires are prohibited and you still insist on using toilet paper, pack it out.

Tampons require extra care. They are often difficult to burn, and campfires are seldom hot enough for complete combustion. For this reason, triple-bag them and carry them out with your other trash. (See an exception to this practice in Chapter Eleven.) Pack them with crushed aspirin or a used tea bag to reduce odor. Under no circumstances should you leave them buried in latrines or catholes for animals to dig up.

Will Waterman

"Natural toilet paper" is an effective solution to one of the most common causes of wilderness trash. It's more comfortable than you might imagine.

Water That Remains

Water used for cooking and dish-washing is another unavoidable waste product. For years, NOLS advocated draining excess water from cooking or washing into the corner of either a fire pit or a nearby sump hole. Upon later investigation, however, we learned that this concentration of dissolved food was another cause of excavation by animals. In addition, if the campsite was a high-impact one, subsequent users often complained of flies drawn by lingering odors. Now we recommend widely scattering such wastewater at least 200 feet from any water source and far from any campsites that are likely to be used again soon. (See Chapter Eleven for an exception to this practice in bear country.) Finally, before discarding your cooking or dish water, always separate food scraps that are large enough to be packed out with your excess trash.

Another use of water in the backcountry is cleaning: Should you use soap or not? Many who advocate using no soap cite the benefit of one less item to carry as well as freedom from concern about dysentery if soap residues are left on cooking utensils. Others can't do without it, stressing both personal and group hygiene. A few advocate compromise—soapless dishwashing and personal bathing, but washing one's hands with soap after relieving oneself.

Will Waterman

When bathing, carry water at least 200 feet from any lake or stream, lather up if you use soap, then rinse off.

From strictly an impact standpoint, the best solution is not to use soap in the backcountry. Soap may alter water's delicate pH balance and may seriously affect aquatic plant and animal life by introducing phosphates and other chemicals. If, however, you can't (or won't) give up soap, you should minimize the chance of soap entering a water source. Always choose a kind that is phosphate-free, and keep it well away from streams and lakes. The best technique for bathing is to carry water an adequate distance from a source. (Your cooking pots or water jugs are convenient containers.) Get wet, lather up, and then rinse off. Again, 200 feet is the recommended minimum distance. This allows your wastewater to filter through the soil and break down before returning to any nearby body of water.

Finally, if your clothes need washing, consider rinsing them, using no soap at all. Besides its polluting effect, soap is difficult to remove from clothing, especially without warm water, and residual soap can cause skin irritation. For these reasons, choose a creek or stream with a substantial flow (not a small body of water) to rinse your soapless laundry, and remember to rinse your underwear far from any water source.

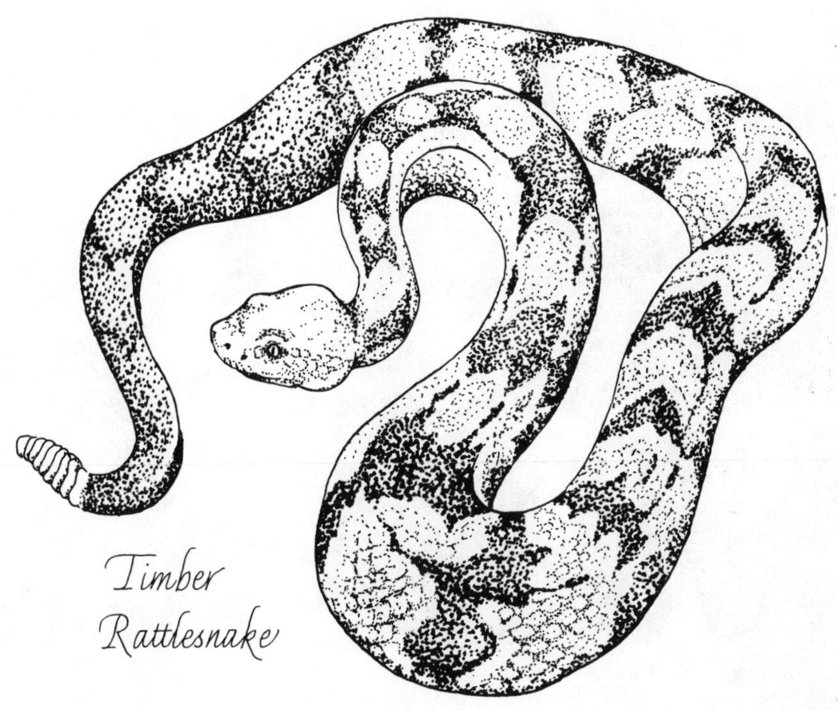
Timber
Rattlesnake

Will Waterman

Special Environments

Someone once likened the North American mosaic of wilderness that ranges from the Arctic to the Tropics to a grand play made up of many different acts. Each act represents a special kind of environment, and the multitude of plants and animals that inhabit each are a special cast of characters. If this analogy is accurate, then it follows that the conservation practices we've discussed so far allow us only a general view of the plot. Although our basic practices are appropriate in most cases, applying a single, universal technique to every situation doesn't always work.

Special environments imply special techniques. Yet often we lack knowledge of human impact on different landscapes. In the following chapters, this realization is painfully obvious. Most studies have been done in forests and mountains and are of a more general nature; few have addressed impact in the specific environments of rivers, coasts, or snow and ice. Although these landscapes may present special problems, they also suggest unique opportunities: tides and floods rejuvenate our impact on shorelines; snow offers us extremely durable campsites; travel on rivers enables us to carry out our waste.

Common Loons

This way of looking at these environments gives us hope that there are solutions to the special problems they present. The important question we must always ask is this: Will we humans be viewed as a major character in these wildland environments, or will we play only a minor role? Our answer should always be the same. As visitors, we must reduce the changes we impress upon the land to a bare minimum, allowing natural processes to find their own part to play.

Will Waterman

Chapter

Six

Deserts

Desolate, forbidding, worthless—this has long been humankind's view of desert lands. Hardly more than a few generations ago, Daniel Webster asked, "To what use could we ever hope to put these great deserts and those endless mountain ranges?"

Today, thousands of desert travelers could answer Webster's question. As mountain trails become ever more crowded, recreationists are discovering the solace of arid lands. With nearly one-seventh of our planet's land surface classified as arid, it's still possible to discover vast areas relatively untouched by humanity. Even though North America's deserts are relatively small, constituting only 8 percent of the world's total desert area, they are geologically young and biologically diverse, and they abound in recreational opportunity.

There's no precise definition of where a desert begins and ends; the distinction between arid and semi-arid is seldom clear. Yet the common denominator is dryness. Early meteorologists considered any area receiving less than ten inches of precipitation per year a desert. Now we realize that other factors besides rainfall—evaporation, high radiation, fierce winds, and soaring ground temperatures—contribute to dryness. Still, we have difficulty defining the limits of desert in all but extreme words. We know that true desert is a harsh land—slickrock, sand dunes, arroyos, and canyons—that is immutable, permanent, and indelibly etched into the surface of dry, hot earth.

Although we're beginning to see a stark but raw beauty in this arid country, its ruggedness demands closer inspection. What we find is not a land hardened to any and all abuses we may throw its way. Because of the scarcity of water, vegetation, and organic soils, desert lands are particularly susceptible to damage. In fact, with the exception of alpine and arctic tundra, the effects of backcountry use are more severe, more noticeable, and

Banner-Tailed Kangaroo Rat

longer-lasting in dry country than in perhaps any other environment.

The Stark Desert Landscape

Before we can learn how best to minimize impact on this landscape of extremes, we must develop an understanding of how desert ecosystems work. In particular, we must recognize the unique nature of the desert's vegetation and soils.

Looking over the vast expanse of desert, most visitors are impressed with its sterile and lifeless appearance. Barren ground is more abundant than vegetation, and rock and sand more common than soil. A closer look, however, reveals that deserts are very much alive. Most desert landscapes consist of dispersed islands of life and fertility in an ocean of barren rock and mineral soil. Although the in-between areas are mostly sterile, these islands of vegetation, animals, and dry organic soils can be as diverse and teeming with life as more moist environments. The reason the land looks so stark is that these islands occupy only 10 to 20 percent of the ground surface—an adaptation to the absence of water.

Water is the key to patterns of life in the desert. Because it severely limits productivity, plants must be particularly careful to conserve water in an arid climate. During frequent dry periods, desert plants accomplish water conservation by cutting back on growth. Thus, slow growth and competition for water result in the characteristically sparse vegetation of the desert—vegetation that's often the product of centuries of development.

One can hardly look at the barren expanses between desert vegetation and not wonder how plants could grow, for what we normally think of as healthy soil seems absent from these arid lands. Mature soil is a blend of both live and decaying organic matter, mixed with disintegrated rock, and separated by air and water occupying the spaces between soil particles. By this definition, our first impressions seem right: Most desert soils are far from rich in organic matter. Given the low productivity of desert vegetation, it's not surprising that decaying organic matter is in short supply. Yet there are places, under trees or shrubs in the vegetation islands, where organic matter is abundant.

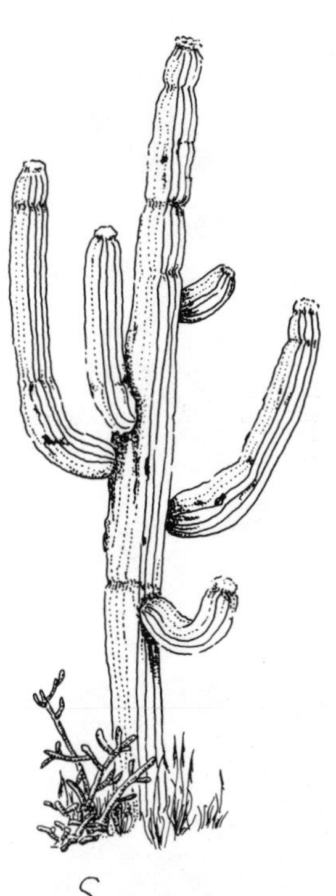
Saguaro

Topographic features of deserts also affect vegetation and soil patterns. In mountain and plateau country, bare rock is extensive, forming cliffs and areas of rock outcrops called slickrock; soil and vegetation are mostly found along dry washes and arroyos. When rain falls, water sweeps down these drainages, depositing much of the material brought from the land above. In North America, these raised surfaces along lower elevations are called bajadas. Soils on bajadas are generally quite coarse, and vegetation grows well here because coarse soil has large spaces between particles to hold air and water. Finer materials take longer to settle and wash down into undrained basins, called playas, at the base of bajadas. Vegetation is sparse in playas because the fine-textured soils allow little air and water to soak into the ground, making it difficult for plants to survive. Here, water remains close to the surface—so close, in fact, that after heavy rains, playas may temporarily become lakes. Since large volumes of deep groundwater are rare in deserts, because of infrequent rainfall and high evaporative rates, it's this water- and air-retaining capability of soil that influences patterns of desert life.

Will Waterman

Arroyos, water channels filled with mineral soil and subject to occasional flash floods, offer resistant travel paths.

Water as Life-Giver

Water is the lifeblood of the desert. After a heavy rain, bare limbs sprout new leaves, and a brief but glorious bloom of wildflowers may cover normally barren soil. Where water funnels into washes and arroyos, floods rip out smaller vegetation trying to establish a foothold. Larger shrubs and trees often survive floods because their root systems are stronger and able to reach the water supplies beneath the surface of dry washes.

Occasionally, permanent water is available in the desert. It may occur at springs along a fault line or where a stream flows into the desert from higher elevations. In effect, these are nondesert environments superimposed on the arid landscape. Where plants have access to permanent water, they grow luxuriantly, and riparian zones teem with life. These streams and water holes provide a focal point for desert wildlife. They also attract humans who not only need the water to drink, but also enjoy the shade and more familiar landscape that the existence of permanent water brings.

Life on the Dry Side

Human use affects several important aspects of desert life. First, many of the characteristics that allow desert plants to survive, such as thick leaves or sharp spines, make them hard to damage. For this reason, we think of most desert vegetation as quite resistant; it's tough, durable, and capable of tolerating considerable abuse. Once plants are damaged, however, they have little ability to recover; although their resistance to damage is high, their resilience is low. This is a reflection of the low productivity of desert vegetation. Despite the initial resistance of the cacti and shrubs of the desert, many are hundreds of years old. Once they are damaged, centuries may pass before their richness is restored.

Riparian zones respond oppositely. These rich ecosystems are more similar to humid environments far from the desert. Generally, the resistance of riparian vegetation is lower than that of vegetation in the neighboring desert, but its resilience is high. Human impact in riparian zones may be readily obvious, but damage is often short-lived, either because of vegetative regrowth or because of the rejuvenating effect of periodic floods.

Will Waterman

In elevated desert areas, slickrock provides durable cross-country routes if you avoid places where soil is forming.

Choosing a Route

As desert travelers, we must recognize the complex association of water and soil, which in turn affects conditions favorable to desert life. Our actions should give this life the best chance for survival. The landscape may be tough, but it's also fragile, and we must choose our paths of travel carefully.

Where are the places we'll have the least impact? The dispersed desert growth pattern provides abundant opportunity for us to concentrate our activities on the more sterile spaces, avoiding the fertile islands of vegetation and rich soil. Often, these places are already established by trails, and in popular desert areas, they remain the best choice. Still, established trails are scarce in remote desert areas, and cross-country travel may prove the only possible means.

Traveling on the exposed mineral soil of playas often causes the least impact simply because fewer plants struggle for existence there. Although sometimes more circuitous, sandy washes or arroyos also provide good travel paths. In permanent stream bottom areas, where more moisture is available and regrowth is faster, vegetative damage is usually not long-lasting.

If you hike along elevated areas, try to stay on slickrock and avoid vegetation. Keep your group small, walking abreast to avoid compacting a new trail in places where soil is forming. Remember—as this soil wears away and soil granules pack closer

Will Waterman

The mosses, algae, lichens, and fungi of desert cryptogams are extremely sensitive to trampling.

together, it has less ability to hold the water needed by existing and future vegetation.

Soil That Isn't

When choosing bare ground areas for camping and hiking, desert users must watch for another feature—fragile cryptogam soils. Derived from two Greek words meaning "hidden marriage" and unique to desert ecosystems, cryptogam looks like exposed mineral soil with a dark, thin crust. Underneath this crust is what at first appears to be only soft and lumpy soil. Close inspection, however, reveals a spongelike structure, which is really the home of a combination of mosses, algae, lichens, and fungi. A self-sustaining biological unit requiring little nutrition from the soil, it grows on barren ground as a pioneer species. A critical part of the

Will Waterman

By following an established trail through cryptogam, these hikers are creating the least amount of disturbance.

desert soil-building process, cryptogam's anti-erosional and nitrogen-enriching abilities prepare the ground for a succession of future plant communities.

A mature cryptogam garden may take as long as 100 years to develop, but can be destroyed by just a few steps, turning into dust that blows away with the next windstorm. David Cole's study in Grand Canyon National Park found that as few as fifteen people walking over an area of cryptogam pulverized more than one-half of the crust. This is the most fragile ground cover ever reported, and yet it's quite common in many desert lands. If you find yourself in a cryptogam area, stay on established trails or, if there's no way to avoid the cryptogam, follow in each other's footsteps in order to create the least disturbance. (Note that this is counter to the general practice of spreading out

NOLS

Ancient Anasazi artifacts of the Southwest are in increasing danger from curious backcountry visitors as well as thieves and vandals.

when traveling cross-country—a practice best suited for crossing less fragile terrain.)

The Facts About Desert Artifacts

Modern-day backcountry travelers aren't the first people to find value in desert living. Early Americans of the Anasazi culture flourished in the Southwest about 1000 A.D., then mysteriously disappeared a few centuries later. Many archaeologists consider the Anasazi to have been almost as advanced as the ancient Maya in Central America. Today, all that is left of this ancient agricultural civilization are their cliff dwellings, pictographs or petroglyphs, and scattered artifacts, such as bowls and pottery. Now these are quickly disappearing because of theft and vandalism. Despite the threat of stiff fines and prosecution, land managers have been unable to stem the desecration of these ancient ruins. By some estimates, fewer than 10 percent of these valuable artifacts remain.

If you come across ancient dwellings in your wanderings, whether in the desert or in other environments, show your respect by leaving them alone or by exploring them only with great care. Don't camp in these sites or take any artifacts. Many of these dwellings haven't been inventoried or researched, and your disturbance will cheat others of their heritage.

Desert Horned Lizard

Campsite Selection and Use

Little is known about campsite impact in the desert, although there's a sizable body of literature on other arid land damage, especially that caused by off-road vehicles. It seems safe to assume, however, that the conclusions we've drawn about the complex interaction of desert soil, water, and vegetation also hold true for those places where our concentrated impact is greatest.

In Chapter Three we stated that established camps take up a considerable area. Campsites in deserts are generally much smaller, sometimes averaging only a fraction of the size of campsites in forested backcountry. Why the difference? First, the smaller size of campsites in deserts is the fortuitous result of a hostile environment offering few comfortable places to camp; the terrain is often rough. Second, desert camping is a relatively recent phenomenon; most areas have little or no history of deleterious "frontier-style" camping.

Desert Tortoise

A third reason for smaller campsites is the inherent resistance of desert vegetation. Although few plants survive in the core of most desert campsites, the area immediately adjacent to this barren core remains relatively undisturbed. In comparison, the disturbed area surrounding campsites in more temperate climates is often nine times the size of the campsite core. Rugged plants that have evolved in the harsh desert environment resist trampling by humans. Annuals complete their life cycle in a time period sufficiently short to avoid most recreational use. Drought-enduring perennial species have small leaves with thick cuticles and are often armed with thorns or spines that keep most users away. Finally, many above-ground arid plants are small in proportion to their large root systems, making contact with the plant less likely.

All this may be good news for desert campsites, but resistance of vegetation to trampling is only half the story. On forested campsites in moister environments, there's usually a lag between the time a campsite first loses vegetation and when it finally loses its organic soil. On desert campsites with little organic soil, however, exposure of mineral soil occurs almost as rapidly as plant cover loss. Thus, although the area of disturbance in most desert campsites is small and desert campsites may absorb much visitor use, once they are damaged, recovery is extremely slow.

What does all of this imply for desert backcountry users choosing campsites? In low-impact desert areas, a pristine campsite is a good choice provided it has no vegetation and is a highly resistant environment—for example, slickrock, dry washes, and even open ground between shrubs if there's no cryptogamic crust. Remember to keep your group size small and your stay short, and disperse your camp activities over a wide area. In popular desert areas, or when you can't be certain that you'll leave no evidence of your stay, a high-impact campsite still remains the best choice.

Fires

Because of the low productivity and scattered growth of vegetation, campfires are often impossible in the desert; there's simply not enough wood for fuel. What little deadwood does occur is often critical to nutrient cycling in those soils already low in organic matter.

With this in mind, it's easy to conclude that campfires have no place in the desert. For the most part, this is true. In arroyos, however, periodic flash floods often deposit substantial amounts of driftwood and flood debris. It's important not to overuse this limited fuel supply, which seems locally abundant but may not be replenished until the next flash flood, sometimes years away. In addition, when you are collecting driftwood for a campfire, it's easy to confuse driftwood with live wood. Trees or shrubs in arid regions often appear dead, when, in fact, they are naturally dry and brittle.

Provided an adequate wood supply is present, campfires may be appropriate for yet another reason. Dry desert washes often have abundant mineral soil, making these suitable locations for campfires; no rocks are blackened, no vegetation is trampled. In the morning, the ashes can easily be dispersed. Just covering the remnants of your campfire with sand is not good enough; wind will blow the sand away, and the less dense charcoal and ashes will "float" to the surface. Remember to grind up any larger pieces of charcoal before scattering them over a large area. Although charcoal from natural fires is relatively common in many forested areas, such is not the case in deserts, where any leftover charcoal is almost always a sign of previous camping.

Utah Juniper

Sanitation

Since there is so little organic matter to provide sustenance for the microorganisms that eventually break down fecal material, sanitation in the desert presents a problem. Body waste won't decompose in this predominantly inorganic, often sandy soil, but instead dissipates, filtering through the ground as it follows natural drainages. In this respect, distance from water may be more critical than whether you bury your feces or deposit them at the surface. Choose a site not only far from water, but also far from any major potential drainage such as arroyos or gullies, or in shallow soil on slickrock.

Because deserts are hot and direct sunlight is pervasive, surface disposal is acceptable in remote areas that have small likelihood of discovery. Fecal pathogens are readily destroyed in such conditions; surface-deposited feces, however, are likely to re-

Will Waterman

Water is the key to desert life, and backcountry visitors have an obligation to protect this limited resource.

main visible for a long time in the desert, where the air is dry and little rain falls to dissipate them. Insect contamination of surface deposition isn't the problem it is in more humid conditions, but direct visual contact is. Like the scar created by an ill-placed campfire, desiccated human feces will be obvious to other visitors for a long time.

The best method? Because the sun's heat penetrates desert soils, shallow catholes are usually more appropriate than surface deposition. Visual contact by other visitors is kept to a minimum, and high temperatures near the soil surface (as high as 150 degrees Fahrenheit) destroy pathogens in a relatively short time. Not all burial methods work in the desert, however. Here, latrines are even less acceptable than in temperate climates, for burial deeper than a few inches eliminates the sterilizing effect of the sun's heat. The number of microorganisms is so low, and aeration is so reduced because of the compact nature of many desert soils, that deep, concentrated burial only preserves solid waste.

Water

A discussion of arid country is not complete without a few cautionary words about water. In deserts where running water isn't available, a spring, seep, or water pocket is often the only supply for miles. It's critical that visitors not pollute, over-consume, or waste this valuable water; it is a finite resource.

Desert Bighorn Sheep

Camping close to water is probably more appealing in the desert than in any other environment, but you should avoid camping directly next to water unless you're in an area where it's abundant. Your distance will lessen encounters with other parties that might be drawn to the source. Even more important, it will allow wildlife access to water. Herein lies a problem that most desert visitors fail to consider: A water source may be only a convenience to us, but local animals depend on it for survival. Camping near a water source may keep away wildlife that is wary of people. Always camp well away, and avoid using this source after dark; most desert animals are active at night, often concentrating around water.

When you use desert water, conserve it. It may only exist because of a lucky combination of shade, a small drip, or an occasional flood, and because inflow and evaporation are in delicate balance. Judge your type and volume of water consumption by the replenishment rate. Use small water pockets for drinking only. Springs may have enough water for you to use for washing dishes (far from the source), and flowing streams may have adequate supplies for washing clothes and bodies. Use only clean cups or pots to dip from sources; even clean hands transfer some salt and oil into water.

Remember that there are few mechanisms for replacement or purification of these limited water sources; hence, pollution is cumulative. Overconsumption or misuse on your part will deplete water for all forms of desert life.

Will Waterman

Chapter

Seven

Rivers and Lakes

Water belongs to earth. Or perhaps more correctly, earth belongs to water. Outside of earth, water is solid ice or invisible vapor; only here is it found in the liquid form available for carbon-based life reactions. If earth's orbit were 1 percent larger, scientists speculate, its water would have frozen more than 2 billion years ago; 5 percent smaller and it would have boiled away. Yet water is more than just the basis of life as we know it. Water transports the molecules necessary to life through leaves of plants and bodies of animals. It also forms into raindrops and puddles, rivers and streams, finally washing to the sea. On its way, water carries life to the most remote of places.

Human travel on water to gain access to wild country is nothing new, but its current popularity is. When John Wesley Powell slid his dory into the Colorado River in 1867, he could not have imagined the recreation explosion that within a hundred years would bring so many others to that same muddy river. In the first eighty-three years after Powell's descent down what many call the greatest river in the world, only eighty-five people followed—an average of one person each year. Between 1950 and 1970, people "discovered" the Colorado. In 1972 alone, more than 16,000 people traveled through the Colorado's Grand Canyon. Even with the present limit on numbers, the 300-

mile float remains one of the most intensively utilized wilderness resources in the world. The demand for this experience is so great that some people wait as long as a decade for a private trip through the canyon.

What does backcountry travel on rivers and lakes and along coasts have in common? We travel in craft that allow us to carry more gear—something that may be good or bad for these environments, depending on what's brought and what's left behind. In addition, use of water craft concentrates our impact along a narrow strip of land—the river, lake, or coastal shoreline. Finally, this narrow strip of land is usually both resistant and resilient, a quality we rarely see in other wildland environments.

The Way of Rivers

When those of us who live inland from the coast think of water, we often think of rivers. Our language reflects respect: the "mighty Mississippi," the "wide Missouri." Yet of all forms of water—oceans, glaciers, polar icecaps, lakes, groundwater, and atmospheric moisture—none takes up less volume than rivers. Only one-millionth of earth's total water actually flows within the banks of rivers. Still, our respect for the moving power of rivers is great; rivers are deeply ingrained in our past. We first explored the land traveling up and down their liquid highways, defined boundaries by their watersheds, and finally farmed their rich alluvial valleys. If the sea is where we came from, as author David Quammen has said, then rivers are how we got here.

It seems we need rivers for more than just commerce. In 1977 a hefty 16 percent of the total United States population—nearly 28 million Americans—participated in some form of canoeing, kayaking, or river running. Projected popularity by the year 2030 places white-water boating almost 300 percent above present levels, second only to downhill skiing. Although river running's popularity has increased dramatically, America's rivers suitable for backcountry recreation are hardly meeting demand. Of the 3 million linear miles of rivers and streams in the United States, only 7,000 miles were classified in the National Wild and Scenic Rivers System in 1986—a meager 0.2 percent. Perhaps of even greater concern, we are just beginning to learn how to care for our wild riverine environment.

River Otters

Rivers as Water Trails

At first glance, river use appears to be the nightmare of all possible backcountry situations—a large number of visitors traveling along a single thoroughfare. Yet compared with travel on land, rivers can absorb much visitor use and still afford each user a high degree of solitude.

Backcountry visitors who hike seldom start at the same place or move in the same direction. Rafters or boaters on a river, on the other hand, usually begin their trip at a single location and travel in only one direction—downstream. If a group of ten people floats ten miles each day and there are nine other such groups, each starting at the same place a day apart, every group can have a relatively unique and private wilderness experience. How many environments exist where a hundred people can crowd onto one trail, travel ten miles each day, and be assured of not crossing paths?

Although the social impact of seeing few visitors may be less on river trips, the environmental impact can be significant. Seldom do river users venture much beyond the shoreline. This means that even though the surrounding backcountry may be quite large, camping is concentrated. Often, campsites are few in number because of the ruggedness of a river corridor, or because camping is allowed only in designated sites. Or they may simply be favorite locations. Although a river shoreline may be "cleansed" by periodic flooding, and regrowth is relatively rapid, repeated camping severely hampers recuperation of these sites. As in popular mountain or desert wilderness, the major part of

Bruce Hampton

The best river camping areas are beaches, sandbars, and nonvegetated sites somewhere below the high waterline.

the river corridor may remain scenic and even pristine, but intense campsite use gives the area a feeling of overuse.

What can you do as a river traveler to lessen camping impact? If campsites are regulated, obey the regulations. Usually these areas restrict camping to a few selected high-impact sites that you would normally choose anyway. If campsite selection is not regulated, follow the decision-making process discussed in Chapter Three. Base your choice on the amount of use the area receives, the size of your group, and your ability to select a resistant site. In most cases, the best location is on the floodplain of the river. River users can camp on beaches, sandbars, or nonvegetated sites—somewhere below the high waterline. When the river floods, footprints wash away, and the site appears "new" to the next user. If you practice this floodplain camping, your impact will always be minimal.

Ground above the floodplain is less desirable because impact won't be so easy to disguise. Still, it's not always possible to avoid these high-ground locations. Dam-controlled rivers may flood daily to their high waterline, a heavy rainstorm may threaten a rapid rise in water level, or the high waterline may be so close to the edge of the river that your camp may visually affect the experience of other boaters. In these situations, it's better to choose a high-ground campsite, preferably one that's both safe and screened from other users. If the river is popular, it will most likely have a number of high-impact sites from which to choose. Camp in these sites, and avoid creating new ones.

River Campfires

Pull into a campsite on a sandbar or beach on a popular river, and you're likely to find little firewood. Past campers have stripped trees of deadwood, and the floating driftwood you saw in the last upstream eddy is absent. You're glad you brought your stove.

Firewood along rivers is becoming increasingly scarce, especially on rivers controlled by dams. Only limited flooding occurs now (or not at all), and once-abundant driftwood no longer periodically flushes through the river corridor. But dams aren't the only reason for the scarcity of firewood. Even where rivers flow free, driftwood is disappearing. River campers are burning up this finite resource more rapidly than it's being replaced.

One answer to the problem is to bring your own wood or charcoal if you must have a fire. Extra weight and space are generally not a problem in a raft or canoe, and this is a simple solution for a few nights of campfires on high-impact rivers. Nonetheless, you must still decide where to build the fire and what to do with the ash afterward. Conscientious boaters carry fire pans, portable containers in which the campfire is built and the ash confined. Garbage can lids, oil drain pans, barbecue

Will Waterman

On remote rivers where fire pans are deemed unnecessary, always build campfires just above the waterline. The sand or gravel provides a durable surface, and when the river floods, all evidence will be washed away.

grills, small barrels cut in half, and steel baking pans all make good fire pans. Generally, sand or exposed mineral soil is common in most river campsites, and the fire pan can be placed directly on this surface.

Even when you use a fire pan, what to do with leftover charcoal and ash presents another problem. Traditionally, these fire leftovers were scattered over the campsite, buried in the sand, or dumped into the river. With increased use, however, and because of the confined nature of many campsites, these practices aren't satisfactory today for high-impact rivers. In popular campsites, such practices have darkened many beaches, and charcoal can be found twenty or thirty feet from existing fire pits. Another method—throwing charcoal and ash into the river—removes floating fire remnants from one beach and deposits them in an eddy downstream. Although these practices may suffice in a truly pristine river corridor, fewer such rivers will exist in the future.

One reliable method of charcoal and ash disposal is to pack it out. Let the fire burn down overnight, and place the cool ashes in an airtight surplus ammo box. These remains, if placed in the next night's fire, will continue to burn down so that the box rarely fills up.

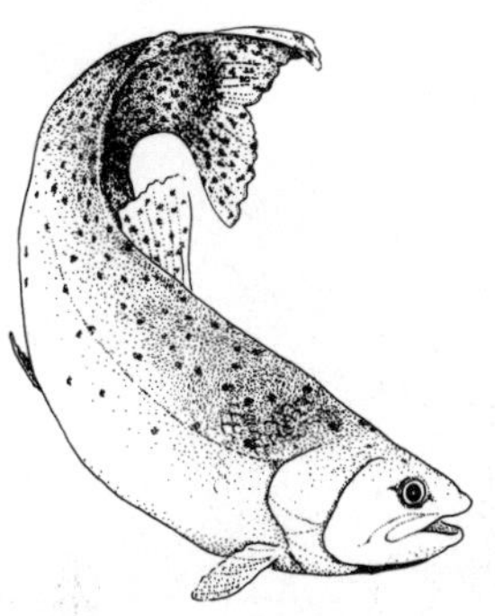
Cutthroat Trout

River Sanitation

Human waste is another serious problem river travelers face, because both sides of the shore drain directly into the river. Burial or surface disposal well away from water may suffice along remote rivers, but is simply inadequate on popular float trips. Especially critical are arid regions where rivers have cut narrow canyons, organic soils are minimal, and campsites are few.

The solution devised by river runners for popular rivers without toilets is to carry out all solid human waste. The equipment needed is a waterproof surplus ammo can, several large heavy-duty (5-mil) plastic garbage bags, chemical quicklime or Chlorox, and a toilet seat.

Here's the procedure. Line the ammo box with one or two plastic bags, folded over the rim. Place the seat on top. Cover the box with a spare bag between uses to keep out flies. The chemicals are added before and after using; they keep the smell down, and retard decomposition and the production of methane gas, which could explode the bag once it is sealed. Don't urinate into the bag; urine greatly increases the volume of waste, makes handling difficult, and dilutes the chemicals and reduces their effectiveness. Place toilet paper directly into the bag. Before traveling each day, squeeze the air out of the bag, then close and store it in the same box (or another) with the previous day's bags. When this system is used with a larger-size surplus ammo box, seventy to ninety person-days of solid waste can be contained within one

Bill Petersen

A surplus ammo box makes an effective portable latrine for traveling on rivers or lakes where disposal of human waste is a problem.

box. At the end of your trip, deposit the waste in an appropriate landfill.

Urine is another difficult problem along rivers because of its concentration in high-impact campsites. Where there's little rainfall to dissipate it, the offensive odor of urine tends to linger. Urinating away from a camping area usually solves this problem, but the outskirts of your camp may be the kitchen or sleeping area for the next party. Therefore, always go far away from camp, and choose a location that will clearly not be a campsite, lunch spot, or rest area for someone else.

Recently, another solution to urine disposal has become popular, particularly on large western rivers: urinating directly into the river or wet sand along the shore. Advocates of this method suggest that the high volume of water will adequately dilute small amounts of urine. As discussed earlier, however, urine may not be the sterile by-product it was once thought to be and, in certain human populations, may harbor resistant pathogens. Unless specifically suggested for the river you're floating, we do not recommend this practice.

Trash and Wastewater

Trash shouldn't be a problem on a river trip, even though there's usually more of it than on a backpacking journey. What isn't burnable can be carried out in a garbage bag or a surplus ammo box. All extra food should be carried out, not scattered. Some river users even spread a large tarp on the ground and eat their meals there in order to catch any food particles that may otherwise litter the site. This practice is especially useful when camping in a high-impact campsite that you suspect will soon receive more visitors.

Yellow Monkeyflower

Wastewater from cooking and bathing demands extra attention at high-impact river camps. Small amounts of leftover cooking water shouldn't be scattered at the edge of the campsite, but deposited directly into the river. Pour the cooking water through a fine mesh screen to remove the larger food particles. (Bag these particles for packing out.) Microorganisms found in rivers rapidly break down the minute food particles that pass through this screen filter. Scattering the wastewater, particularly in dry climates, will attract flies and add to the existing odor problem.

When bathing with soap, you should follow the general practices outlined in Chapter Five, making sure you are at least 200 feet from the river and any side streams or creeks. If possible, choose a site with organic soil. In most rivers of heavy flow (not small streams), it is appropriate to take an initial dip in the river to wet yourself, then retreat an adequate distance before soaping and rinsing. This wastewater doesn't usually attract flies, and even though soap may not be broken down completely before it filters into the river, it will seep in slowly.

Lakes

Lakes differ from rivers in several important ways. The ease of traveling in many directions creates difficulty finding solitude, a problem typical of other types of backcountry. Relatively constant

Bruce Hampton

Low-growing willows just above the shoreline on this Alaska lake show heavy trampling damage. If previous users had camped on the gravel shore, as these visitors are doing, the site would still be pristine.

water volumes mean there's little opportunity to camp on a spot that will be rejuvenated by yearly floods, as is the case along rivers. Thus, camping practices are more similar to those described in Chapter Three. Finally, driftwood is less common, resulting in a situation similar to riparian environments. On the other hand, travel on lakes often permits one to carry more gear than on rivers. Therefore, unless portages are too demanding, the caring user will bring a fire pan and will consider, on popular lakes, bringing ammo boxes for charcoal and human waste.

A Final Caveat

Simply because of increased demand and limited supply, many of our remaining wildland freshwater recreation areas are highly regulated by land management agencies. A future list of wilderness rivers and lakes won't include many new additions to what we have now; already, managers of an increasing number of rivers require that each night's campsite be reserved months in advance. In this sense, as use expands, recreational river and lake management may portend much of what we should expect in the future as our favorite forests, mountains, and deserts become ever more crowded. It's important to be meticulous in our treatment of wildland rivers and lakes if we want to maintain their ecological integrity and still ensure an enjoyable experience for the many people following us.

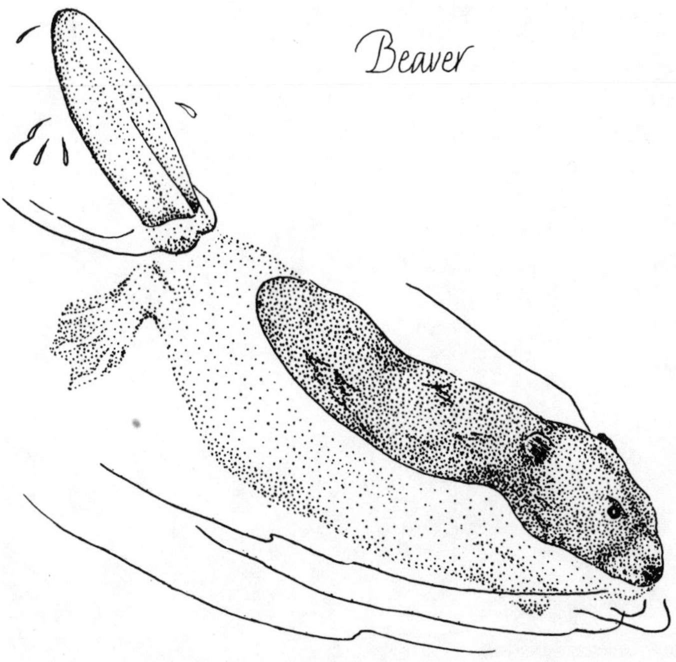

Will Waterman

Chapter
Eight

◆

Coasts

◆

As a result of the search for wildland that is relatively free from growing numbers of recreationists, coastal boating and camping are increasing in popularity. And it is no wonder, for along the contiguous United States there are almost 37,000 miles of shoreline; along Alaska's coast there are more than 47,000 miles. Altogether, nearly 66 percent of America's coastline is under public ownership (mostly in Alaska). Add the coast of Canada, Mexico, and Central America, and the opportunity for secluded backcountry recreation is considerable.

Interest in coasts may be growing, but coastline impact is still poorly understood. Moreover, coastlines are too diverse to be easily characterized; the cool, wet hemlock forests of coastal Alaska are quite different from the hot, dry desert shores of Baja. We should expect our impact and our conservation techniques to vary accordingly.

Where the Sea Meets the Land

The Tlingit Indians of Alaska used to believe that tides resulted from a battle between the moon and the raven. The raven wins a narrow strip of land from the sea in order to feed his brother animals, only to lose it again as the daily battle ebbs and flows.

Although we tend to think in other terms today, two aspects of this legend still ring true: the narrow strip where the sea meets the land has long been a fierce battleground, yet it's an extremely fertile region, highly productive and teeming with life compared with many other environments. This fertility of the intertidal zone results from the rapid cycling of nutrients, in the form of large quantities of detritus (organic wastes and dead matter) produced by the constant battering of wind and waves.

Western Hemlock

Because the intertidal zone is subject to regular flooding, coastal shorelines, like those found along rivers, make good campsites. But here the similarities end, for coasts are far more durable and resilient following disturbance than are riverine environments. Flooding occurs each and every day, and many of the organisms that have adapted to coastal life are hardy enough to resist most of the impacts associated with backcountry use. Thus, though it's true that coastal camping concentrates use along a narrow strip of land, the constant rejuvenating effect of wind and waves makes seashores among the least sensitive areas available for recreation.

Still, use is rarely restricted just to the intertidal zone and those beaches that extend inland for short distances. When we travel or camp beyond the line reached by tides and storms, we must be aware that life in these areas is more sensitive and easier to disturb. Therefore, it's important to concentrate as many activities as possible on resistant coastlines and to use the areas beyond with special caution.

Coastal Camping

At present, few of our remote coastlines receive enough recreational pressure for impacts to be widespread. There are notable exceptions, particu-

Will Waterman

larly where unsuitable terrain physically restricts campsites to only a few popular locations. Given the resistance and resilience of sites along the coast, however, it should be easy to maintain the pristine character of our coasts if we're mindful of what makes the most acceptable campsites.

Camping above the daily high-tide line but below the monthly high-tide line guarantees minimum impact, as does cooking in the daily intertidal zone.

The absence of vegetation and organic soil in the intertidal zone and inland beaches means that there's little disturbance caused by human trampling. Sand isn't very compactable, and neither pebbles nor gravel shows much sign of a past tent site or cooking area. Therefore, where intertidal beaches are abundant—even in popular areas where recreational use is quite heavy—it is appropriate to choose campsites where it appears no one has ever camped before. There's no need to worry about either concentrating or dispersing tents or traffic routes as long as activities are confined to resistant surfaces. These campsites can be used repeatedly and for long periods with little adverse impact, even by large groups.

Although it isn't always convenient to confine all camp activities to the intertidal zone, it's often possible to limit most use within this zone, then choose a sleeping site above the high-tide mark. On most beaches, high tides leave a distinct line of debris and occur twice daily, about twelve hours apart. Over a period of a month, tides will be the highest near the time of both a new moon and a full moon. Sleeping above the highest daily tide, but below the monthly high-tide mark, guarantees that all traces of your campsite will soon be washed clean. Resistant sites may be found above monthly high-tide lines, but evidence of your stay won't be removed as rapidly.

If it's necessary to camp entirely off the beach, follow the general guidelines presented in Chapter Three: Decide whether to choose a pristine or a high-impact site, select a resistant location, and behave in a manner appropriate to the site you select. Be careful not to locate your campsite in sand dunes that are in the early stages of formation. Here, sparse vegetation is just becoming established and is particularly vulnerable to trampling. Destruction causes accelerated wind erosion, which can alter the beach and dunes. Generally, sites in grass are more resistant than those vegetated with low-growing shrubs.

Fires on the Beach

When firewood is abundant, locate campfires in sand, on rock, or in nonvegetated mineral soil, preferably within the daily intertidal zone. But be cautious about using driftwood; replenishment is unpredictable and highly periodic along many coasts. What seems like enormous quantities of driftwood today may disappear tomorrow because of displacement of storms or use by other visitors.

A situation requiring special care in gathering firewood is Alaska's extensive "ghost forests," created by the Good Friday earthquake in 1964, when vast amounts of coastal land subsided, allowing saltwater to inundate what had been healthy forests. The resulting groves of dead trees now bear stark testimony to this major force of change, so active along the West Coast. In some popular camping areas, these groves show signs of excessive fire building by thoughtless campers. Carry a stove so you won't be tempted to further damage such places where driftwood supplies are scarce.

Disguising a fire site is easy along the coast if you always build the fire in sand or beach gravel, or on a flat rock. Scatter the ashes and any leftover charcoal directly into the sea; wave action will soon destroy evidence of your fire. If you're camping in a popular area that may soon have other visitors, pulverize your charcoal to hasten the process.

Humpback Whale

Sanitation

Like both campsite and fire site selection, human waste poses few problems in most coastal environments. It's a simple matter to urinate below the high tide line (away from tidal pool areas), where the ocean soon dilutes urine. In general, the usual criteria for selecting a method of feces disposal apply: surface deposition above the tide line is acceptable in remote areas where there's little chance of subsequent discovery; catholes are appropriate where discovery is likely or organic soils are present. Since soil microorganisms are most prevalent in environments of moderate temperature and moisture, the above-tide line soils of mild coastal climates usually provide relatively rapid decomposition if you choose the cathole method.

Before assuming disposal above the high tide line is the only alternative, however, consider the marine environment; bacteria that break down fecal material are usually abundant in the intertidal zone. In one coastal study by Paul Godfrey on Cape Cod, bacteria were 1,000 times more numerous within the intertidal zone than in the sand above high tide. This suggests that the sea may be another place to deposit your body waste *if* the coast is remote. The recommended method in this case

Will Waterman

Depositing human waste on a rock and then throwing it into the sea is acceptable in remote areas with no tidepools.

is to deposit your waste on a flat rock, then throw it out into the water, well away from your campsite. If no rocks are available and the area is infrequently visited, use the beach at low tide. When using this method, remember that beaches with waves and strong tides are best for breaking up and dissipating fecal waste.

A new sea disposal technique with considerable potential for popular areas involves a variation of the portable latrine method outlined in Chapter Seven. In this case, line the surplus ammo box with heavy-gauge paper (*not* plastic), have all party members deposit their feces in the lined box, then sink the paper and feces far offshore on the next travel day.

Since little is known about sea disposal of any kind, use these techniques cautiously. Weigh your decision to deposit your fecal waste into the marine environment against the impact of catholes and surface deposition on the surrounding land above high tide, and the frequency of use along a particular coast. Potential ecological problems with this method include the introduction of pathogens and toxins into the marine environment through uptake by various filter-feeding organisms. Also, an immediate concern is ingestion if visitors use saltwater for cooking. Although these possibilities exist mostly with large amounts of waste, we don't know enough to rule out problems with smaller quantities. Consider the movement of water through waves, tides, and currents; deposit feces off points in deep water with a strong current, or on beaches with abundant wave action. Make sure that you aren't introducing waste into calm water along beaches that have little natural flushing, in tide pool areas, or in shallow water with productive shellfish beds. Always avoid popular areas where others may be swimming or snorkeling.

Green Turtle

Disposal of Other Wastes

With few exceptions, proper disposal of trash, garbage, and wastewater is also somewhat easier along the coast. If you're traveling by kayak or canoe, in most cases you have extra space, and carrying out your unburnables presents no problem. In remote areas, however, where your trash will only end up in a town or village that has no proper community landfill, sea disposal may make more sense. Although such "littering" appears to run counter to a wildland ethic, the alternative of carrying your trash back to civilization, where it may be dumped somewhere other than an appropriate landfill, is clearly worse. Nonaluminum cans may be dropped far offshore (one-half mile or more) into deep water after paper has been removed and the ends cut off. The cans soon rust, and bottom-dwelling organisms will find useful homes in the meantime. Throwing these items into the water from shore is not acceptable; wave

Sea Otter

action will only wash them onto the beach. If you use this sea disposal method, be aware that it's only appropriate when carrying out garbage or trash offers no better solution. Under *no* circumstances should you deposit plastic into the ocean or use this disposal method in estuaries or freshwater lakes.

Will Waterman

Where the coast is devoid of tidepools, deposit wastewater from cooking and washing in the intertidal zone, where bacteria will soon render it harmless.

Pick up any litter you can. In particular, plastic litter should always be packed out. Plastic doesn't degrade rapidly and often floats, tangling and killing unsuspecting birds or mammals. Be especially conscious of plastic six-pack holders and monofilament fishing line; these often ensnare diving birds and can harm young birds when used as nesting material.

Avoid leftover food by carefully planning your meals. If small amounts of leftovers remain, scatter them far offshore in the same manner as cans. Scavenging birds are abundant in most marine environments, and a small amount of leftover food deposited far from shore is little reason for concern—unlike other backcountry environments, where wildlife habituation to human food can alter critical feeding habits. Fish remains can be disposed offshore in a like manner. Depositing these on shore is less acceptable, especially in frequently visited areas.

Excess cooking and bathing water rapidly breaks down if it's deposited where bacteria are most common—in the intertidal zone. Be aware, however that tide pools are particularly susceptible to water pollution; avoid depositing any kind of wastewater in these locations. If the area is free of tide pools, scattering wastewater in the daily intertidal zone allows soap and leftover food particles from bathing or cooking to sink into wet sand, where bacteria soon render it harmless. If you deposit this leftover water directly into the sea, a thin surface film may form, unless there is enough wave action to dissipate it. In remote areas that have few visitors, bathing in the sea with a biodegradable soap is an acceptable alternative to confining all washing and rinsing to the intertidal zone. Nevertheless, this is an unacceptable practice where large groups repeatedly use the same site, where wave action is nonexistent, or in areas of rich tide pool life. Remember that it's always best to minimize the use of soap and to avoid depositing sizable quantities in any water environment.

California Gulls

Wildlife Disturbance

Wildlife is more abundant along coasts than in any other environment. It's difficult to travel where the sea meets the land and not be tempted to explore, photograph, or even harvest some of these animals.

Islands accessible to canoes and kayaks deserve special attention because island ecosystems function differently from mainland environments. Often, their isolation has brought about the evolution of unique organisms, endemic populations of rare plants and animals. Because they've evolved under conditions of infrequent disturbance, these organisms may have little inherent resistance and are particularly susceptible to human disturbance.

Approach large concentrations of birds and sea mammals with caution; when they're nesting or birthing, avoid them. A single unwitting visitor has been known to destroy an entire bird colony's hatch by frightening adults at a critical time. Exposure of eggs to heat or cold may result in chick mortality if nests are abandoned for long. In the case of seals or sea lions, a major factor in infant mortality is stampeding and trampling by adults. In both these situations, it's better to approach from an upwind direction and stay in view to alert the animals early on of your presence. At the first sign of restlessness, back off. Staying a discreet distance away allows one to observe these animals in a natural setting and may avert a calamity.

Northern Sea Lions

If you must get close to a colony to obtain a photograph, minimize the potential for disturbance by choosing an isolated nest or animal at the edge of the rookery. Get in and out quickly, preferably without leaving a trail; predators sometimes follow human scent. Some researchers even say that the disturbed path visitors make through

Will Waterman

Approaching coastal wildlife by boat is generally less harmful than walking along shore because it alerts animals early on to your presence.

grasses alerts airborne predators. Gulls have been known to follow humans, pouncing on eggs or nestlings as soon as the adults leave. Approaching animals by boat is generally less harmful than such shore-based activities as walking or camping close to nests. Perhaps the best advice is to shoot your picture with a powerful telescopic lens, thus avoiding any disturbance in the first place.

Changes in the behavior of large marine mammals caused by human recreational activities range from playful curiosity to significant agitation. In Glacier Bay, Alaska, C. S. Baker and colleagues studied the reactions of both humpback whales and harbor seals to small boat traffic. Both species showed deviation from normal behavior, although the overall impact was hard to assess. Certainly, disruption of these animals' feeding habits could be stressful. Where human traffic is frequent, the added stress may cause some sea mammals to go elsewhere.

The harvesting of marine organisms should be given careful thought. If fishing, catch or spear only what you can eat. When diving, restrict your hunting to areas with abundant sport fish, and try to select a variety of species rather than just a few favorites. If you return to the area often, monitor the population. If many people fish there, it's probably a good indicator that you shouldn't.

White Pelican

Shellfish are particularly affected by overharvesting. Collect only from areas with abundant populations; practice random harvesting rather than cleaning out one area entirely. When clamming, replace smaller clams to ensure future generations. Fill in any holes after digging; juvenile clams and other tidal flat organisms are sensitive to changes in the depth of their sand covering.

If you harvest crabs and lobsters, select only the larger specimens, and take only the males. It may be increasingly popular to catch lobsters by hand to give them a sporting chance, but try not to injure or break an antenna, then lose the lobster; such injury can result in its death.

Keep in Mind

Because coastal ecosystems are so bountiful, many indigenous people still live by the sea. Besides your environmental impact on the land and your social impact on other visitors, you often have a cultural impact on native people. It's common courtesy to seek permission before photographing natives or trepassing on native land. In places where artifacts are present, leave them undisturbed; if removed, they will lose much of their meaning. Treat these people's history and culture as an intrinsic part of the surrounding landscape—the same landscape that belongs to a people who first discovered a world where ravens battled the moon.

In the feeble light between the drawn-in houses of a winter village, you can hear the breathing of something with ice for a heart.
—Barry Lopez, from *Arctic Dreams*

Joel Rogers

Chapter

Nine

Alpine and Arctic Tundra

It's not coincidental that some of the places most attractive for wildland recreation are those least attractive as permanent living places. A frosted alpine meadow in Wyoming, the windswept arctic tundra of Alaska—what do these environments have in common? Cold. It has discouraged human use of the land, at least enough to forestall the dense settlement found in more temperate climates. Cold, and the human desire to avoid it, has given us much of what today we value as wilderness. It's the land no one wanted—until now.

Although most of us may not wish to reside permanently above timberline or to live buried in the darkness of an arctic winter, our summer recreational use of these cold environments continues to grow. As more benign landscapes become crowded, we find open space and fewer people in these areas. A pattern has emerged: Not long ago, we first ventured into high mountains; now we travel into distant northern lands of arctic tundra. Although recreational use of most of these fragile landscapes may not yet be comparable to more popular lands below timberline, as use increases, so will our impact.

How do alpine and arctic environments compare with others? If impact depends not only on how durable an environment is, but also on how soon it may recover once it's damaged, then alpine and arctic tundra are perhaps the most fragile of all.

Peregrine Falcon

Low temperatures and harsh conditions—a short growing season followed by deep snow, low light levels, and freeze-melt cycles—combine to force tundra plants and animals to adapt to a rigorous environment. Like desert vegetation, some tundra plants produce tough foliage capable of withstanding challenges brought on by cold. Often, these adaptations are the same qualities that protect the landscape against human damage. Nonetheless, just as the absence of moisture prevents deserts from healing rapidly once damage occurs, cold preserves impact by extending the time required for recovery. Cart tracks left in 1819 on Melville Island in the Canadian Arctic by a British expedition are still visible today. With this in mind, our primary goal in this fragile backcountry is to recognize and utilize resistant areas, reducing the lengthy recovery time to a minimum.

Because they're so similar, it's difficult to separate the above-timberline tundra environments found at high altitude from those of high latitude. In fact, most of the arctic tundra used by recreationists is also mountainous. Many of the same species of plants and animals inhabit both ecosystems, bearing testimony to a time not long ago when much of North America was covered by vast sheets of ice. Although the following discussion of alpine and arctic tundra is separated for the sake of convenience, many of our specific recommendations apply to both.

Alpine Lands

If cold is the limiting factor affecting high mountain environments, then we should be able to follow cold's transition and see its effect on the land. In North America, this alpine environment is found in numerous places: close to the coast, inland on the continent, rising from the desert, at the North Pole, or even in combinations. What all these environments have in common is the tendency for cold to preserve moisture in its solid form; the higher

David Cole

one ascends, the longer snow persists. Likewise, as we climb, we see a dwindling amount of vegetation, until finally we reach a place where trees are scattered and dwarf-like—a place biologists call the "kampfzone" (zone of struggle), in recognition of the severe conditions that trees face at high altitude. Above this zone, trees disappear into low-growing alpine vegetation. Near the summit lie deep snowfields; summer hardly reaches this land before winter follows once again.

Biologists call the area near tree line the kampfzone, *the zone of struggle, in recognition of the severe conditions life faces at high altitude and latitude.*

To minimize our impact on this vulnerable landscape, we must first recognize that people are simply an unnatural part of the alpine environment. Unlike those in temperate lands, plants and animals in alpine areas evolved largely in the absence of people. As the popularity of alpine recreation grows, no longer is this true. For instance, Glacier National Park, which is well known for its high-altitude environment, has received more than 26 million visitors since 1910, almost half of them during the past decade. Plant communities—usually the first to show signs of disturbance—may be adapted to their severe physical environment, but not to the onslaught of human visitors.

Concentrated patterns of human use have a further impact on vegetation and soil found at high altitude. The greatest number of visitors are usually present at the peak of the alpine growing season in July and August. Trampling stresses life at a time when plants are most vulnerable. Moreover, visitor impact is influenced by the total number of people and whether they travel on trails or cross-country.

Alpine Traveling

As at lower elevations, most alpine visitors choose to hike on trails rather than strike off cross-country. This is generally beneficial to alpine plants and soils because trails restrict trampling to just a few locations. In many areas, however, trails don't go to all the places people want to travel. Also, lack of brush and tree cover at high elevations sometimes makes cross-country travel easier than at low elevations. Consequently, more people venture off trails, trampling places that have never felt boots before.

Although leaving the trail can alleviate crowding, it often aggravates environmental problems—loss of vegetation, damage to soils, and disturbance of wildlife. In alpine areas where recovery is particularly slow, damage can be serious. Once informal trails develop, the likelihood is great that others following will make things even worse. Soon, webs of trails crisscross formerly trailless areas, pristine basins become scarred with tent sites and fire rings near timberline, and wildlife moves on in search of ever-fewer undisturbed ranges.

Responsibility in alpine areas is the same as anywhere off-trail, but the consequences of poor judgment are much more severe. Once vegetation is lost, erosion removes already-thin topsoil, making recovery extremely slow. Working in Colorado's Rocky Mountain National Park, scientists Beatrice Willard and John Marr suggested that complete recovery of alpine tundra disturbed by informal trails would take from several hundred to a thousand years—even if it was never used again. If we employ all of our horticultural know-how—planting, mulching, and fertilizing—we can't cause these places to recover quickly.

On Washington's Mount Rainier, researcher Ola Edwards uncovered a troubling story about heather meadows, a common but fragile part of many alpine landscapes. Once an opening develops in the heather cover—something that happens after a plant is stepped on just a few times—the plants are unable to close the hole by spreading vegetatively. This minor disturbance initiates an irreversible cycle of erosion. Needle ice, which forms as a result of daily freezing and thawing, lifts up the soil, subjecting it to erosion. With the shallow roots of heather exposed, death soon follows. Small bare spots become ever-larger, and if they are abundant, the result is destruction of meadows, some of which are estimated to be at least 10,000 years old.

This scenario may seem extreme, but it's not unusual. Seemingly innocuous changes—changes that are minor in more resilient environments—can thwart highly specialized means by which plants and some animals adapt to the harsh alpine climate.

Pika

Although the consequences of poor judgment when traveling off-trail are severe, many places in the alpine zone are highly resistant to impact. Where routes are on bare rock or snow, the effects are negligible. Dry meadows are surprisingly resistant; grasses and sedges tolerate moderate trampling because soils are held in place by dense fibrous roots. Even here, however, it's important not to step on any place too often. It is best to travel in a small party, spreading out and avoiding places where it's apparent others have gone before.

Take particular care when ascending or descending steep slopes, or when crossing areas of water-saturated soils; both are common at high elevations. The most critical places to avoid when traveling off-trail are moist ground and steep slopes covered with soil or vegetation, particularly low woody plants, such as heathers, huckleberries, and dwarf willows.

Although it is always easier to minimize damage by traveling on trails, some care is also required here. Late-melting snowbanks and the muddy soils created shortly after they melt must frequently be crossed. As mentioned earlier, it's better to cross snowbanks and mud holes directly than to enlarge the trail system by skirting them. If you find this difficult, perhaps you should consider a lower-altitude trip or visit alpine areas either earlier or later in the year. It's especially important to stay on trails through meadows. Parallel ruts— as many as eleven wide in some places—scar many alpine meadows. Even where parallel trails are not yet obvious, walking alongside the established trail causes damage. In Glacier National Park, for example, researcher Ernest Hartley detected trampling-caused changes in vegetation as far as thirty-three feet beyond the path, a direct result of hikers' not staying on trails.

Alpine Campsites

Many of the same cautions mentioned in alpine traveling apply to camping at high altitude. The inability of campsites to recover is illustrated in another example investigated by Ola Edwards on Mount Rainier. In sparsely vegetated, boulder-strewn areas, campers have moved rocks to create more comfortable tent sites. Unfortunately, the plants that grow here can only survive in the microhabitats around these stones. Once the stones are moved—a seemingly innocent act—a permanent scar is created.

Too many of our high valleys and lake basins are already covered with heavily impacted campsites.

Will Waterman

The most resistant alpine campsites are found on either snow or rock.

The sad fact is that these sites won't recover unless they remain completely unused, whether they're properly used after damage occurs or not. You can use these high-impact sites and not cause further impact.

Camping on a pristine site, in contrast, demands much more care. Choose a resistant surface with no evidence of previous use. Snow, ice, rock, and mineral soil are best. Dry grass meadows are moderately resistant; communities of low shrubs or succulent plants are quite fragile. Often, it's possible to concentrate most camp activities on a hard surface, such as rock or snow, even if you must sleep on a more fragile site.

If your camp activities can't be confined to a hard surface, disperse your traffic widely, trying not to step on the same places. Avoid fragile plants, and don't use the area more than one night. If traveling with a group of more than a few people, separate into several groups, and don't congregate in one location, unless it's a hard surface. No alpine vegetation can tolerate being stressed for long; everything you do on a pristine site should minimize the number of times vegetation is trampled.

Punk Is In

Campfires may be impossible in the highest alpine areas, but their scars are often common at timberline. Here, it's easy to see that past campers could have reduced their impact by a judicious use of stoves instead of fires. But there's another reason campfires are out of place where cold limits the growth of trees. In many tundra environments, forests simply cannot produce enough litter to support both frequent campfires and healthy soil.

Forest productivity studies show that energy is allocated to stems, branches, leaves, and roots, which intercept light, water, and nutrients. Also, energy goes into the production of litter, which supports decomposers and returns nutrients to the soil for the growth of future trees. A healthy forest needs both processes.

Scientists have learned that the proportion of energy bound in leaves, small twigs, and branches, all of which are annually discarded in the form of litter, decreases with increasing altitude and latitude. Forests surviving in intense cold near the Arctic Circle or pushing against the snow line on Mount Hood are not only poor producers, but relatively little of their energy goes into the production of litter. In these cold climates, both the visitor searching for firewood and the soil necessary to future forests are competing for the same resource.

What does this mean to campfire builders at timberline? Since so much of a subalpine forest's energy is stored in wood itself as opposed to annually discarded leaf and twig litter, sending that wood up in smoke deprives future vegetation of one of its main sources of energy in the form of decayed organic nutrients. Timberline campfires short-circuit this critical energy cycle. Our recommendation? Use a stove.

Mountain Goat

Sanitation

If the problem with human waste disposal in the desert is soil that is poor in organic matter because of low productivity, a similar problem exists in tundra ecosystems. In this case, however, low productivity is more often a result of cold than of a lack of water. Although the limiting factors of temperature and moisture may differ, the effect upon decomposers that thrive in organic matter is similar: low productivity limits soil microorganisms. As a result, both deserts and cold environments tend to preserve buried human feces.

For the same reasons that surface deposition is recommended in many desert areas, it may also be appropriate in tundra. Surface deposition offers a tidy solution to digging a cathole in vegetation that may not soon recover. But tundra, particularly alpine tundra, is often popular backcountry. Consider the trade-off between burying feces to avoid discovery by others, and thinly smearing it on the surface, where the sun can decontaminate it and rain can wash it away. Although disposal sites in popular areas may be limited, far up a side canyon or along the bottom of a rocky ridge may provide an adequate location. Stay away from trails, and select a location as far from water as possible. If you bury your waste in a cathole, choose a location away from water, with as much organic soil as possible. Be especially cautious, however, not to excavate vegetation.

Always choose latrines as an absolute last resort in tundra; a large pile of feces will decompose at an incredibly slow rate in cold and sterile soils. If your group is large, the area is popular, and surface deposition or catholes are inappropriate, choose a less popular route or campsites that have toilets.

Arctic Tundra

If alpine areas in the Western Hemisphere were the last to see permanent settlement, then those of high latitude were some of the first. Alaska was inhabited 10,000 years ago, yet its borders contain some of the most wild country, with nearly 70 percent of all national parks and over 60 percent of all designated wilderness in the United States. Include Canada, and a substantial part of North America may be considered available for wildland recreation. As more visitors discover these high-latitude lands, we have a unique opportunity to avoid some of the disturbances so commonly found in more mild backcountry areas.

Although not all northern landscapes experience the harsh conditions associated with extreme cold, it's the land of highest latitude—the arctic tundra—that is most vulnerable to impact. In many ways, the same precautions taken in alpine areas apply to arctic tundra. Yet, if there's a distinction between the tundra of the temperate latitudes and the tundra of the northern latitudes, it lies in the soil: Much of the arctic ground is perennially frozen.

Here, a mixture of underground ice and soil—"permafrost"—lies just below a thin surface layer of soil, which thaws with the approach of summer. As snow and ice near the surface melt, water moves down through the previously frozen soil until it meets underground ice. In most other places water passes into gravel and porous rock to be stored underground, but in the Arctic, water remains pooled above this permafrost barrier. Water literally has nowhere else to go, so it saturates the thin layer of thawed soil. These water-saturated landscapes are extremely fragile, adding an even greater need for caution.

Traveling in the Arctic

It is difficult to walk on arctic tundra during the summer without getting your feet wet. Few trails exist in this part of the world, and cross-country

Bruce Hampton

Permafrost is permanently frozen soil found below a thin layer of surface soil, which thaws as summer approaches.

hiking is often the only method of travel. Nonetheless, visitors prefer to travel on dry surfaces where they find them. Since dry, raised ground is so uncommon, and spreading out is difficult because of low but thick vegetation, cross-country hiking tends to concentrate on relatively few routes, along which informal trails quickly develop.

Damage to the fragile lichen-rich communities that are common at high latitudes is often serious. Lichen colonies are old—some, many hundreds of years old—and inhabit drier ground that is less subject to permafrost. Because they grow in mats and are not rooted to the ground, they're easily disturbed. The actual "leaves" of lichens are brittle when dry, and break rapidly. Finally, their low productivity makes recovery extremely slow; when lichens are disturbed, recovery rates of thirty-five to seventy-five years are common.

Dave Kallgren

In arctic tundra, the best and often easiest travel routes are along gravel streams subject to periodic flooding.

Another impact on tundra is that which happens to the underlying soil after plants have been trampled. As warmth increases with the onset of summer and the top layer of frozen ground thaws, long-dormant plants begin to thrive in the constant light. If vegetation is damaged so that the surrounding soil is exposed, a strange phenomenon begins—thermokarsting. Sun warms the exposed soil more rapidly than ground insulated by a normal covering of plants; more and more surrounding soil begins to melt. Soon, the critical balance of frozen to unfrozen soil is upset, and erosion takes place, resulting in extensive damage.

Where should you walk in arctic tundra? Perhaps the best route is along streambeds. Since water isn't easily absorbed into tundra soil, small amounts of rain cause rapid runoff in natural drainages. Often, the absence of vegetation along the gravel shoreline of tundra streams reflects this frequent flooding. Here, boots do little damage to either soil or plants. If travel on vegetated tundra is unavoidable, choose ground that has few lichens, and spread out to minimize trampling.

Camping in the High North

Like traveling in arctic tundra, choosing a campsite can be difficult. Since dry sites are scarce and damage takes so long to heal, select campsites with care. Botanist David Cooper recently noted how quickly extensive damage occurs. Four visitors camping in a lichen area in the Brooks Range of Alaska for ten days created a disturbed spot of more than twelve square yards; the disturbance eroded the lichen stand to bare mineral soil. Cooper observed that recovery time will be longer than seventy-five years because the damage took place at an elevated location where conditions are particularly harsh.

The best campsites are those that cause the least disturbance to soils and vegetation. They shouldn't be located in or near lichen-dominated stands, nor should they be sited in plant communities subject to thermokarsting. The edges of gravel streambeds make excellent campsite choices as long as you're aware that flash flooding is a possibility. You should also realize that camping in wide valleys found along many arctic streams makes you more visible to other travelers; keep your camp out of sight, if possible, and remember that sounds carry farther in a landscape where trees are few or nonexistent.

When streambeds are unavailable, look for mineral soil sites on mildly sloping land. On many tundra slopes, soil slippage is a common occurrence. You can camp on flat ground, just below the spot where the slow-moving soil will eventually override your campsite in a few years, removing all traces of impact.

Arctic Sanitation

If you guessed that surface disposal is the preferred method for much of the arctic environment, you are correct. Most areas see few visitors, and the long hours of summer sun, coupled with the alternative of damage to tundra vegetation, make surface deposition an easy choice. Take care, however, when choosing a site. Remember that water seeks the lowest level in the surrounding landscape and is seldom absorbed into frozen soil. Always choose a spot well away from stagnant marsh or bog areas where your waste may concentrate.

In more popular areas where contact by others is likely, use a cathole—preferably in unfrozen, organic soil where damage to vegetation is minimal. If no such site exists, choose the ground just below a mound of soil that will soon undergo natural slippage, making sure it's a site no one will soon choose for a camp. In tundra valleys where large rivers have cut meandering, braided gravel beds and visitor use is too frequent to risk surface disposal, bury your feces in a cathole just below the high-water mark. Small fluctuations due to summer rain will probably not raise the water level high enough to uncover your cathole, but the high volume of runoff in early spring will dissipate your solid waste at a time when visitor use is low.

Bristlecone Pine

Will Waterman

Chapter
Ten

Snow and Ice

From our examination of alpine and arctic tundra, we know that cold shortens the growing season, preserving impact by extending the time required for recovery. When the period of cold is relatively short, the land survives mild forms of disturbance. As the period of cold lengthens, however, we know that impact is increasingly difficult to conceal. Although this is particularly true once damage has taken place, those landscapes that suffer periods of prolonged cold—harsh winters or extreme altitude or latitude—often have a protective coating that makes them durable to impact. Here snow dominates the surface of the land for at least part of the year.

It's difficult to speak of cold without mentioning snow. For whenever the mercury in a thermometer begins to plunge and storm clouds gather, we know that precipitation in the form of snow is usually not far behind. It may fall on us during summer if we are high on a mountain glacier, or while skiing through a forest in winter. Cold brings snow; the cold makes the land less resilient once damage occurs, but the snow makes the land more resistant to damage.

Seasonal Snow

For a number of experienced backcountry visitors, winter is a special time. A noisy, crowded wilderness in summer becomes a quiet, empty landscape once snow falls. This, along with the rapid growth of cross-country skiing, may be why winter wildland use is growing in popularity. In Great Smoky Mountains National Park, Bill Hammitt and his co-workers found that winter visitors actually prefer winter over summer; most mentioned solitude and experiencing the winter environment as major factors in their choice. Most avoided backpacking during summer because of heavy use by other visitors. Another interesting finding in this study was that winter visitors are often old hands, averaging at least ten years of backpacking experience. From such studies, we may conclude that as people become expert in the ways of wildlands, they'll find traveling the winter backcountry even more appealing.

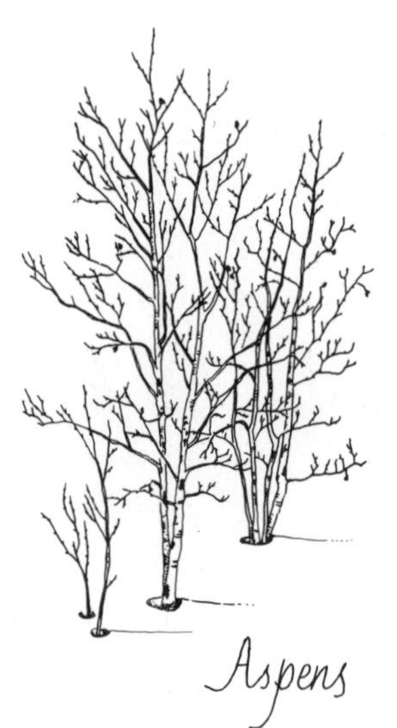
Aspens

Travel in Winter

The small number of visitors and the protection a thick mantle of snow provides to underlying vegetation and soil alleviate some concerns. Because so few visitors are present, it's not as crucial to maintain a low profile. Brighter-colored clothes and equipment aren't a visual impact on others, and may even be desirable from a safety standpoint. There's also little concern over whether travel is along established routes or far from existing trails; most effects will be hidden by the next snowfall or the spring melt.

So what are our concerns in winter? Probably the most important is wildlife disturbance. In certain instances, as when species desert an area entirely, wildlife disturbance is much more significant than are the obvious but highly localized impacts to vegetation and soil that occur along trails, campsites, and other areas of frequent use. If we lose the animals from wilderness ecosystems, we'll lose a critical part of what makes wilderness so valuable in the first place.

Like humans, wildlife find winter a particularly challenging and stressful season. Unlike humans, however, animals don't have sleeping bags to ward off cold and conserve energy; they must somehow

NOLS

find food and shelter under deep snow or in windswept areas. Finally, large animals can't travel on top of snow; they must plow through it, using tremendous stores of energy when they travel long distances. Most animals employ a strategy of energy conservation: They limit their energy needs by minimizing their activities, including searching for food and escaping dangers. Clearly, this strategy is upset when animals are disturbed by recreationists. Flight or fright (both of which are associated with an increased heartrate) increases energy consumption, and the need for more food quickly arises. Acquiring this food often involves searching and traveling—activities that further drain energy—and can institute a vicious cycle of increased demand and stress. Although this may not be a serious problem for a healthy animal in a normal winter, it may be damaging for animals

Disturbance during winter affects animals at a time when they are particularly susceptible to stress; thus it's important to maintain a critical distance.

that are pushing the carrying capacity of their ranges, or during extremely harsh winters.

To avoid such unnecessary disturbance to wildlife during winter, don't approach animals closely. Although this distance is variable both between and within species, most animals won't become overly excited or flee unless approached within approximately 100 yards. Use your best judgment, but always retreat at the first sign of animal restlessness.

Limited research also shows that animals are as likely to be upset by one person as by many people. This suggests that disturbance should be less if a large group stays together; fewer wildlife–human encounters occur with one large group than with many small groups. When encounters with other people in winter are unlikely, keeping a group together is preferable to dispersal. (Remember that the most valid reasons for traveling in small groups are to minimize disturbance to other visitors and to avoid damaging off-trail areas.)

Early- and Late-Winter Concerns

Although a thick snow cover effectively protects underlying vegetation and soil from trampling, a thin and patchy cover renders vegetation and soil vulnerable to damage. When a thin snow cover is compressed and compacted, snowmelt is delayed, shortening the growing season. Even greater impact occurs where snow-free soils, saturated with meltwater, are trampled. Such soils become highly compacted and muddy and begin to erode. Plants pressed into mud have little chance of survival, just as plants growing in wet soils are easily uprooted by a sliding boot.

Avoid use during this season, or travel at either higher or lower elevations. If this isn't feasible, travel in small groups. Visit either remote places, where your disturbance won't be compounded by others following your footsteps, or high-impact places that have already been disturbed. The main problem with this latter option is that damage to

Will Waterman

popular trails during snowmelt often makes costly repairs necessary.

Summer concerns of trampling and concentrated use are absent during winter when snow provides a resistant surface. The most important goal is to select a site where the risk of water pollution is minimal.

Winter Camping

As in winter travel, the lack of trampling impact to vegetation and soil covered by deep snow permits us to relax many of the camping techniques normally practiced in summer. Most important, select a site that won't disturb wildlife or pollute water supplies, and properly dispose of human waste. Whether the site is pristine or high-impact, there need be little concern for the resistance of the ground surface, the size of the group or length of stay, or the location of tents, kitchens, and traffic routes.

To minimize wildlife disturbance, camp away from winter feeding, watering, and bedding

Will Waterman

Winter snow structures are appropriate . . .

grounds. Avoid water pollution by proper disposal of human waste. If you select a campsite that is far from routes and camping areas used in summer, proper disposal is much easier. This is probably the most important impact-related factor to consider when deciding where to camp.

The inability to bury feces in organic soil because of deep snow or frozen ground, low winter sunlight, and the preservation quality of cold temperatures retard breakdown of fecal material. As in summer, decomposition is most rapid in sunlight. Surface deposition is appropriate as long as there's no risk of water pollution and the site isn't likely to be discovered by others. If this isn't the case, catholes just below the surface of the snow may be your best alternative.

If you use this snow cathole method, keep in mind that your waste will be resting on the ground come spring. Pick a site where no one would

Will Waterman

choose to camp and, most important, far from any immediate water drainage. Often, a thick grove of trees marks a suitable waste site that not only has ample organic soil beneath the snow, but also guarantees that no one will choose such a site for a camp the following summer. Finally, because "yellow snow" creates a visual impact, always cover urine stains with snow.

. . . if they are dismantled after use.

There are several compelling reasons for not building fires in winter. Dead and down wood that is dry is essentially nonexistent, so the temptation is to tear off lower tree branches or to pull wood off standing snags. Moreover, it's extremely difficult to properly dispose of the remains of a fire built in snow. Therefore, fires aren't normally recommended except in an emergency. A somewhat less rigid but still-acceptable policy acknowledges that although usually undesirable, fires aren't likely to cause damage if they're built only occasionally, kept small, and confined to remote places seldom visited during any season. Don't disfigure trees when collecting firewood, and disperse all charcoal and ash.

Anytime you camp in snow, make some attempt to camouflage whatever disturbance you create, unless snow is falling so fast that all evidence will soon be gone. If you build snow structures (for example, igloos, quinzees, and kitchens), it is best to dismantle them when you leave. This is very important in popular areas where others will soon follow. Although snow structures may be appreciated by other winter campers, leaving them intact runs counter to the philosophy of low-impact wilderness use. They provide a reminder that others have been there before, violate the principle of leaving areas as you found them, and may even be a safety hazard for other winter travelers. The only exception to this guideline occurs when there's a high likelihood that you'll return on the same trip *and* you're in an area that is infrequently visited in winter.

Will Waterman

If snow is the only nearby source of water, concentrate cooking wastewater in a sump hole.

Winter Trash

Littering is often more of a problem in winter than summer, especially in backcountry areas that experience heavy snowfall. Here, anything dropped into snow rapidly disappears until the following spring. In this respect, snow gives a false feeling of security when you look around your winter campsite and see no evidence of litter you may have inadvertently dropped. Particularly hard to see against a white background are transparent candy wrappers, ski wax scrapings, plastic bags, and white toilet paper.

In the case of individually wrapped food such as pieces of candy, prepackaging is an easy solution. Remove the wrappers before your trip, and package the candy in a single plastic bag. Keeping track of these plastic bags presents the same problem, but on a larger scale. To our knowledge, all plastic bags used for food are transparent, making food identification simple. Until a manufacturer produces a translucent, colored bag that shows up against snow, winter visitors should be especially mindful of this litter potential.

If clear plastic is difficult to see in winter, toilet paper is even harder. Consequently, some winter visitors take only paper of a darker contrasting color. Regardless of color, however, toilet paper is always difficult to burn in snow. Even when the surrounding snow is cold and dry, the snow soon melts, soaking the edges of the paper and leaving some unburned pieces. The easiest solution is to avoid using toilet paper during winter. Snow—compressed and formed into a compact, oblong shape—provides a sanitary and surprisingly comfortable alternative. Best of all, when the snow melts, no evidence remains.

Subalpine Firs

Two small but increasingly frequent litter problems in winter are dental floss, and ski and candle wax. Like plastic bags, they're highly visible come summer and not rapidly biodegradable. Consider using colored floss and candles; they won't be lost so easily in the snow. Stash ski wax scrapings in a plastic bag, and pack them out.

In most winter camping situations, wastewater is not a problem; it's usually too cold to bathe, and often water is scarce, the only source being stove-melted snow. Any leftover water you may have is from cooking. Scatter this excess wastewater whenever the ground is bare of snow. When surrounding snow is the only source of water, or if others may discover your camp before the next snowfall, concentrate the wastewater in a sump hole, well away from water sources.

As in other seasons, if your cooking results in extra food, always pack it out. This is particularly true of leftover grease. Instead of discarding it in snow, to be found by animals, let it cool to a solid, bag it, and carry it out with your trash.

Permanent Snow and Ice

If one travels far enough toward the polar regions or high enough on some mountain ranges, extreme cold and perpetual snow greet the back-

Moose

country user. Here, snow has accumulated for millennia; moisture has been squeezed and compressed by the weight of each year's snowfall until most of the air is removed and all that remains below the surface snow is blue ice. Where snowfall has been great and much time has elapsed, the ice can be extremely thick. Into this hostile environment, where seasons are marked only by more or less snow accumulation, come humans. These areas, where winter never ends, are not as popular or as accessible as more temperate wildlands. Nonetheless, people have left their mark on the land.

A closer look at visitor behavior in the permanent snow and ice environment reveals some noteworthy contrasts. If winter visitors generally exhibit higher levels of backcountry skills than do average summer visitors, then those traveling to the extremes of snow and ice are often the most experienced. Indeed, at this edge of one of earth's most pristine, yet harsh environments, the price of not knowing what you're doing may be your life.

But the most skilled people don't always practice the best conservation techniques. For if pristine wildlands are defined as places where evidence of people is mostly lacking, then many of the more popular high-altitude environments of snow and ice fall far short. One need only look at the vast amounts of trash and garbage past expeditions have left on Everest, Rainier, and Denali (Mount McKinley). Discarding nearly everything in their pursuit of the summit, large expeditions have littered their way up and down many otherwise pristine mountains. In this environment, where extreme cold tends to preserve anything, including human bodies, the only excuse of users has been that snow will eventually cover their litter. The larger question—like living with the knowledge that there are golf balls lying on the surface of the moon—is whether we have a responsibility to keep these pristine wildlands free from our material excesses.

How do we limit impact in these lands of snow and ice? Because litter is such a problem, we can

NOLS

start by carrying out everything we carry in—spent fuel cans, fixed ropes, tents, extra food, even bamboo wands used to mark climbing routes. Burying these in the snow or dropping them into a crevasse is not acceptable. In some cases, trash discarded into a "bottomless" crevasse early in the climbing season has been known to float to the surface later in the summer, when melting water from a glacier rises to the surface.

Visitors to permanent snow and ice, though often the most experienced in outdoor skills, haven't always practiced the best conservation techniques.

Although many smaller and lighter expeditions conscientiously strive to practice litter removal, one area where they often fall short is route marking. Day-Glo orange survey tape is commonly tied to the tops of bamboo wands. As a result, scraps of tape can be found blowing across a snowfield or glacier. Instead of flimsy survey tape, use red or orange duct tape on the wands. Properly secured, it won't blow away.

Besides litter, there are few impact problems

related to travel and camping on permanent snow and ice. Campfires are not possible, and wildlife is practically nonexistent. The only remaining issue is sanitation; here, the difficulty is body waste left in this extremely cold environment. As always, sanitation problems can be reduced by traveling and camping in less popular places and with smaller groups.

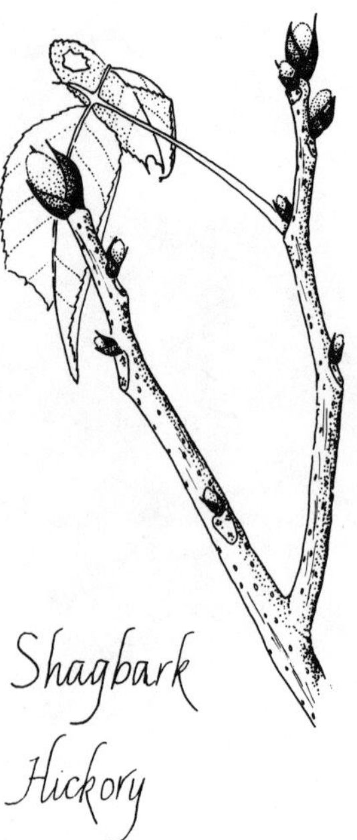

As in winter camping, surface deposition or a shallow snow cathole is entirely appropriate in remote areas or on little-used routes. Another acceptable disposal method is to use crevasses. (On Alaska's popular Mount Denali, this is the approved method.) Unlike trash and litter, which may float if the crevasse fills with water, solid human waste remains at the bottom of the ice. Although little is known about this practice, it is probable that the action of ice eventually moves the fecal waste to a lower elevation, where decomposition or dissipation occurs.

On popular snow and ice climbs without suitable crevasses, latrines have a special function. The concentration of human body waste, which we suggested you avoid in more temperate climates, is acceptable in this cold environment, where we can't expect feces to decompose. Here, it's better to place a group's body waste in one location than to spread it over a large area, where the chance of others' finding it is more likely, and contamination of snow-melted water is increased. Latrines also provide privacy for members of a group. In contrast, scattered catholes and surface deposition offer none.

Lynx

Bruce Hampton

Chapter
Eleven

Bear Country

It is a beautiful summer morning in the most pristine backcountry in North America, with rugged snow-capped peaks, broad forested valleys, meadows filled with elk and deer. You are hiking down a trail. Suddenly, you stop. In the trail lies a pile of mashed raspberries, enough to fill a large bucket. The pile still steams in the cool morning air. You think about it for a moment. Slowly, the hair rises on the back of your neck, and your heart climbs into your throat, beating faster.

Bears!

We may fear them or love them, but above all, we who visit the backcountry respect their power. For the bear is the world's largest land carnivore and one of the few animals that prey on humans. We don't seem able to make up our minds about bears: We have difficulty living close to them, yet most of us don't want to live without them, at least in remote wildland areas. The truth is, this animal that stirs up so many ambivalent feelings among backcountry users is more than just another wilderness species; for many, the bear is *the* symbol of truly wild country.

If a wilderness species is one that requires large amounts of relatively pristine habitat yet possesses a limited tolerance for humans in its wild state, then bears easily qualify. Here is an animal, like elk or moose, that generally does best in the absence of people. As the human presence grows, however, some animals lose their shyness and become habituated to human ways. When this happens, scientists say a species is "behaviorly corruptible."

Unlike the less aggressive elk or moose, once a bear becomes habituated, people won't tolerate its close company. When bears have lost their fear and interact freely with humans, there is danger—not just to humans, but also to bears. In the words of bear biologist Chris Servheen, perhaps a sharper definition of a true wilderness species might be an animal that best lives outside a human-influenced environment and that people refuse to tolerate in close association. If you apply this definition in light of the growing number of recreationists visiting bear country, it's obvious that bears may have more to fear from us than we do from them.

When Bears Meet Man

There are three recognized species of bears in North America: black, brown, and polar. Because polar bears inhabit country that is less accessible to most visitors, the following discussion applies mainly to black and brown bears, and more specifically, the brown bear subspecies considered most controversial, the grizzly. Although our primary concern is how to reduce impact on bears, a knowledge of the different evolutionary paths of bears helps in understanding their behavior when confronted by humans.

The black bear evolved in mountains and forests—areas with plenty of cover and trees. According to Stephen Herrero, author of *Bear Attacks*, when placed in a threatening situation, black bears usually adapt by fleeing or climbing a tree instead of attacking. Still, between 1960 and 1980, black bears injured more than 500 people in North America. Some 90 percent of these recorded bear-inflicted injuries were considered minor, however.

Grizzly and polar bears evolved in high plains and open meadows, tundra, and polar ice, with virtually no place to hide. Their best defense became a good offense, and herein lies the problem: They are unpredictably aggressive.

Compared with black bears, grizzlies at first ap-

Luray Parker

The possibility of changing a bear's behavior once it has learned to exploit human food is remote.

pear relatively benign. Herrero reports that fewer than 200 documented injuries between 1900 and 1980 were due to grizzly bear attacks. Why is this number so low if grizzlies are much more aggressive than blacks? First, most wildland recreation takes place in country that is primarily black bear habitat. Second, black bears outnumber grizzlies by more than ten to one, so the chances of encountering a black bear are much better. Although this may explain the comparatively smaller number of grizzly attacks, it tells us nothing about the severity of grizzly-inflicted injury. Nearly 50 percent of the injuries were classed as major, requiring hospitalization for more than twenty-four hours, or resulting in death.

Aggressive bear encounters occur for a variety of reasons. Perhaps the most common: a bear is surprised at close range, a female bear is protecting her young, or a bear is protecting a food source.

In each of these instances, bears are defending what they deem is rightfully theirs, whether it be space, young, or food. Far less common in wild populations, but more frequent where they've become habituated to humans, are bears that actively pursue people as prey.

Although their life history, habitat, and response to people vary considerably, the three bear species have several basic traits in common: They are long-lived, intelligent, and opportunistic. Because bears have the ability to take advantage of any food source within their environment, once they have exploited human food, they continue to seek it out. The possibility of changing their behavior once bears have received such positive reinforcement is remote. Before 1970, more than half of all grizzly-inflicted injuries in national parks occurred in Yellowstone National Park, where bears had become "corrupted" by feeding at garbage dumps and campgrounds.

From this brief survey of bear behavior, we might conclude that all bears are dangerous and that encounters between bears and people can and do lead to serious injury. There is another side to the coin, however: people-caused injury to bears. When humanity invades their habitat and conflict occurs, bears are heavy losers. Since the settlement of the contiguous United States, the grizzly's population has dwindled from an estimated 100,000 bears to probably fewer than 1,000. When conflict results in injury to people, the bear is often destroyed. For the first eighty years of this century, grizzlies were responsible for fourteen human deaths in the lower forty-eight states. During just five of those years—between 1968 and 1973—180 grizzlies were killed, most close to or within the boundaries of national parks.

Both bears and people have much to gain by mutual avoidance.

Bear Avoidance

The easiest way to avoid bears is to stay away from those wildland areas where bears live. For visitors who fear bears or who fear for bears, this choice is sound and, in specific instances, may have strong merit. This option, however, limits backcountry use to relatively few areas, since bears—particularly black bears—inhabit such a large and varied amount of wildland that a map of their range covers most of North America. Assuming that most visitors want to recreate in lands where bears still roam, the next best choice is to avoid a confrontation to ensure both human safety and a safe future for bears. If your actions are successful, you will see either no bear or a distant one.

Black Bear

Once you make this commitment to avoid bears, your next decision is to know the species of bear you're trying to avoid. Information from the land managing agency, as well as from others who have visited the area, is a good place to start. Perhaps even more important, learn whether the area has a history of bear-people conflict. Then evaluate the potential for a possible encounter, choosing a level of avoidance that lessens the chance of confrontation. Hiking the Appalachian Trail in the Great Smokies, where you may expect black bears to be habituated to human food, requires a level of precaution that you may choose to ignore in Colorado, where black bears are normally aloof and secretive. The level of avoidance should grow in relation to the potential for conflict; backpacking Alaska's coastal tundra, where you may encounter both polar bears and grizzlies, calls for the highest level of bear-avoidance techniques.

In the following discussion, we assume a worst-case scenario. You're in backcountry that harbors bears habituated to humans, or you fear that an encounter may produce some unpleasant results (to you or the bear), or both. Sometimes our recommendations run counter to practices we advocate in situations where either bears are absent or conflicts with humans are rare. A careful judgment must be made when concern for your safety or the safety of bears outweighs your goal of minimizing impact to other aspects of the wildland environment. Weigh the factors of bear species, the potential for conflict, and the possible consequences of that conflict, then choose the technique that not only best reduces your chance of an encounter, but at the same time harms the backcountry the least.

A Trinity Worth Remembering

There are three general guidelines to lessen the chance of a bear encounter. First, do everything you can to avoid surprising a bear. All bears have a critical space they will defend if they feel threatened. This space varies with environment, time of year, abundance of food, and the individual bear. The critical distance may be as little as a few feet for a black bear, 150 feet for a male grizzly, or as much as several hundred yards for a grizzly sow with cubs. If you're far enough away that a bear doesn't consider you a threat, then your chances for avoiding a confrontation are good. Usually, when a bear gets a whiff of human scent or hears human noise, and is not confronted within its critical space, it quickly leaves.

Second, should you find yourself accidentally inside a bear's critical space, maximize your presence. If challenged with what it perceives as a threat, a bear will size it up and act accordingly. At some point, a bear will flee and not confront the danger; this decision appears to depend on the physical size of the threat. For black bears, one person may elicit a bear's fast retreat; for grizzlies, the more people, the better. Statistics on grizzly attacks show that large groups of people are safer than small ones. There are no documented attacks on parties of six or more persons, and your chances are extremely good even with a group of four people. For this reason, your group should be large enough to ensure some measure of safety if you travel in grizzly country.

Finally, avoid attracting bears. A bear's sense of smell is excellent; they're attracted by food smells and other odorous materials, such as fish, soap, and deodorant. Make every effort to reduce these bear-attracting odors to a minimum, and keep them apart from your sleeping area.

Traveling in Bear Country

When traveling in bear country, you can minimize the chance of a confrontation by avoiding certain seasons, and by planning your route away from specific places where bears are most likely to be found. Bears usually travel far and wide in search of food, and depending on the season, you can make some general assumptions about their presence in relation to food sources. During spring, after a winter of inactivity, a bear often feeds on young vegetation on lower southern exposures, the first ground opened to the sun. In summer, a bear may range from the seashore to above timberline, living up to its reputation as a wandering omnivore, and feasting on everything from dead whales to alpine flowers. Come autumn, abundant berry patches and fish-spawning streams are favorite bear habitat. Often, simply using areas other than these will lessen your chances of encountering a bear. But what do you do if you find yourself unavoidably in prime bear habitat?

Polar Bear

Like people, bears usually choose familiar paths of least resistance. Stay away from game trails through brush or forest, particularly bear trails found along spawning streams, rivers, and berry patches, and through passes on ridge tops. These trails are often staggered oval depressions, as bears commonly step in the same places. Or they may be two distinct lanes, the distance apart of a bear's legs. Don't camp near such trails, or close to human trails, as bears use these too, especially at night.

As you travel in bear country, be conscious of tracks, scat, and mounds of excavated earth where a bear has dug for food. Consider traveling out of the area and camping elsewhere if you see an abundance of these signs. Avoid all carrion or places with the smell of decaying meat; you may be near a bear's food cache. After eating their fill, bears—particularly grizzlies—often cover a kill with dirt, branches, or forest litter, then bed close by. If a grizzly is near its food cache, it will be short-tempered and unpredictable. Stop as soon as you smell something foul, and make a wide berth.

In grizzly country, hiking groups should never be smaller than four people, if possible. Since few grizzly attacks have occurred where people are gathered close together in numbers of four or more, we must assume there's some imposing feature in a group's appearance that deters grizzlies from an aggressive response, even when their critical space is violated. Nonetheless, a group is ineffective if its members are not close together.

Making loud noises along the trail is another way to ensure that you don't surprise a bear. Whistling, singing, ringing a bell, clapping, and loud talking are all effective. These should be used anytime a group enters a forest, brushy area, willow patch, or terrain where visibility is impaired, such as rolling hills or dips in tundra. Never should anyone make noises like a hurt animal or a bear, since these sounds may act as an attractant. Keep in mind that roaring streams mask sounds, so be particularly cautious when approaching one without an open view.

Campsite Selection

When choosing a campsite in bear country, keep away from places where bears are commonly found—their food sources and travel paths. Usually, the best choice is to select an elevated campsite in moderately open country. This practice allows both you and a bear greater chance of detection and less chance for surprise. In grizzly country, it's particularly reassuring to locate your campsite in an area with a scattering of climbable trees. Unlike black bears, grizzlies are less likely to climb a tree. Thick trees and brush, however, only increase the potential for a confrontation.

Where you anticipate bears, especially grizzlies, your kitchen site should determine your campsite. Here, it's best to forgo the normal practice of keeping all food far from water. Locating the kitchen close to running water helps keep the area free of food odors by absorbing and transporting minute food particles and cooking wastewater away from

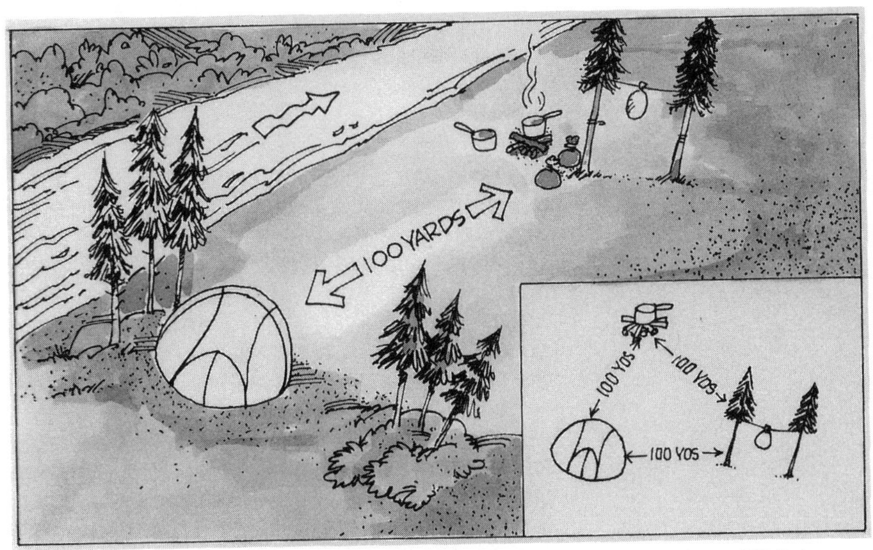

Bill Petersen

your campsite. Designate one general cooking area by a stream for everyone in the group, then position the sleeping area at least 100 yards from this site. If the terrain allows, locating tents out of the streambed and up on a bluff will keep food odors away from the sleeping area.

If camping along the streambed is the only possibility, choose a site at least 100 yards upstream of the cooking area. The usual down-valley winds of the evening will keep food odors from the sleeping area most nights. It's true that up-valley winds of the morning may reverse the process and blow odors in your direction; if a confrontation occurs, however, it's far better if it happens during daylight, when the bear is easily seen. In brushy or flat lowland areas, the camping choices are less clear. Here, you should keep to more open areas and maintain at least the 100-yard minimum distance from your cooksite.

If you're camping along the coast, camp on the beach instead of in the nearby forest. Out in the open, you will have a better chance of forming a group if you're confronted by a bear. Cook close to

In bear country, locate your camp in moderately open country where approaching bears may be readily seen, but with a scattering of possible escape trees. Locate the cooksite a minimum of 100 yards downwind of tents, preferably near water to carry away odors. Suspend food from trees near the cooksite, or store on the ground at least 100 yards from both your tent and *the cooksite. Leave your pack outside the tent with flaps open. (Adapted from* Bear Attacks, *by Stephen Herrero, by permission of Nick Lyons Books, New York.)*

the high-tide line, then sleep at least 100 yards up or down the beach from this area.

In-Camp Techniques

Raven

After setting up camp, practice impeccable camping by keeping all food and food odors separated from your sleeping area. Plan your meals so that what is cooked is promptly eaten. Don't spill food or wipe your hands or utensils on your clothes. The smell of fish or other greasy foods is especially attractive to a bear; minimize their contact with clothing and equipment. Consider cooking in special clothing, such as nylon wind gear, that stays at the cooksite when you're done cooking and can be easily washed. Many people even wear a stocking hat over their hair, since hair readily absorbs food odors. After each meal, wash your face and hands in the stream.

Place all food and cook gear in specified bags, minimize food contact with the rest of your equipment, and keep odorous articles like soap and toothpaste in the cooking area. Remember to transfer trail food from day packs back to cooking sites by nightfall; under *no* circumstances should you keep food of any kind in your tent.

If you've located your cooking site beside a stream, clean utensils of all food particles, rinse them directly in the stream, then bag them with your remaining food. Any minor food residue will be washed downstream. Small amounts of cooking water can also be deposited in the stream rather than scattered widely, as is normally recommended. Use your best judgment as you evaluate the volume and resiliency of the stream. High-volume rivers or streams can withstand direct immersion when you are washing pots; low-volume streams, on the other hand, simply can't absorb this kind of impact. If you choose not to use this method because of possible pollution of the stream, use a sump that concentrates wastewater in one spot and minimizes the spread of odors. Always cover this sump with sand or soil after use.

If you carry canned meat, such as bacon or tuna,

cook and eat it just before leaving camp. Burn the can in a fire to destroy the odor, then place it in a plastic bag and carry it out. Any knife used to clean fish should be kept with other cooking articles, and the fish themselves should be cooked and eaten immediately; don't save them for breakfast. It's best to catch fish away from camp and clean them there. Use the same discretion as in deposition of wastewater. If the stream has an ample volume and the area is used infrequently, throw the viscera back into the water, to be carried downstream. If the stream is too small to absorb this kind of impact, or if the area is subject to more than occasional use, deposit the fish remains at least a quarter mile from camp.

Kinnikinnick

Around camp, always be cautious of bears, even though there may be no evidence indicating their presence. Most experts agree that it's advisable to sleep in tents in bear country. Although no protection against a determined bear, a tent may dissuade a mildly curious one from approaching closer. If you still desire to sleep under the stars, you should always be near a tent, ready to get inside if a bear is suspected in the area. The first person rising in the morning must be particularly alert, and should walk to the cooking area with appropriate noise and a visual check of the area.

If you wander away from camp when scouting for firewood or to relieve yourself, be extra-cautious in grizzly habitat. An excursion near camp is probably safe because of the noise from camp activities, but a longer walk is best made with a minimum of four people.

How to Protect Your Food

Losing food to a bear creates problems for both bears and visitors. The bear may become habituated to obtaining food from humans, making it more likely a confrontation will eventually occur. Moreover, you may have to cut short your trip because your food and perhaps your equipment are gone. In remote areas where access is limited, your survival may depend on these items. Thus, it's particularly important to store them in a location that is as bear-resistant as possible.

Keep your food at least 100 yards from your tent site. In forest or dense brush, the safest storage area is often your cooking area. Food odors are concentrated in one location, and no one risks a trip to yet another place to gather or retrieve the food containers.

Will Waterman

Hanging food high and close to the trunk of a tree usually suffices in grizzly country, but not where black bears are a problem.

Where trees are common, visitors often hang their food out of reach of bears. But if bears are long habituated to humans, securing food from experienced bear "thieves" can prove challenging, to say the least. Where bears are particularly adept, sometimes the managing agency provides a method of protecting food. You should realize, however, that established storage facilities may be indicative of an area with "problem" bears; even these methods may not suffice against a determined animal.

Numerous methods of food-hanging have been devised, from simple poles that lift a container of food high up the trunk of a tree, to elaborate suspension systems hung between two trees. Your choice of methods often depends on the ease of construction and the species of bear. (Grizzlies aren't adept climbers, but their reach is great.) Rigging a suspension system each night is a laborious task, but must be done correctly if you want to protect your food. Get into a routine every day, whether or not fresh bear signs are evident. Always allow ample time at the end of the day to not only cook but also hang your food before darkness falls. The best intentions most often fail when you arrive late in camp and don't properly protect your food.

In bear habitat without trees, food protection isn't as simple. Usually, open country means you're more likely to encounter grizzlies, but often these bears are less habituated to human presence and aren't expecting a handout. Store your food on the ground (wrapping it in extra plastic bags may reduce odors) at least 100 yards from your tent site *and* cooking area. If you place your food bags in separate locations, chances are even better a bear

Bill Petersen

To suspend your food, use about 100 feet of eighth-inch or larger nylon rope. (Adapted from Bear Attacks, *by Stephen Herrero, by permission of Nick Lyons Books, New York.)*

won't discover all the food in one night. It's wise to mix your meals so that all breakfasts or suppers aren't in the same food bag; if a bear discovers a bag, it's less likely you'll lose all of one kind of food. Although this method is not as foolproof as hanging, in open country there are few options. Above all, never sleep with food; it's better to lose your food than to risk a close encounter with a bear.

In recent years, a new product for protecting food has appeared that may make former methods obsolete—a bear-resistant, unbreakable plastic container. Rangers in Alaska's Denali National Park report excellent results when backpackers carry food in this lightweight container with a tight-fitting but removable end. From 1982 to 1987 incidences of bears' obtaining food from backpackers dropped 74 percent. When these containers become commercially available, they'll offer back-country users a more reliable alternative, particularly in treeless bear country.

Sanitation

Like many other animals, bears search out and excavate what humans bury, including feces. For this reason, surface deposition is especially appropriate in bear country, provided all other factors (impact levels, water pollution, direct contact) are carefully considered. In popular areas that are also frequently used by bears, catholes may present the only realistic option; possible excavation by a bear is not sufficient reason to forgo burying feces if you suspect that other people may find your waste.

Menstruation may present a problem for women traveling where bears are common. Recently, in a Canadian laboratory, researcher Bruce Cushing tested polar bears for their attraction to seal scent (the odor of the natural prey of polar bears) and human menstrual blood. Both elicited a maximal response from captive bears. In later field tests, used tampons were detected by polar bears nearly two-thirds of the time. Although these tests are far from offering conclusive evidence that menstruating women are subject to attack by bears, it does suggest that women who are traveling and camping in bear country should use caution. Where black bears are the only kind of bear, the potential danger is much less. But perhaps in grizzly or polar bear country, the best precaution for women is to use tampons rather than pads.

Disposal of used tampons is a problem that is less easily solved. Burial almost guarantees excavation where bears are active, possibly habituating bears to the taste of human blood. Moreover, the usual practice of triple-bagging used tampons and packing them out with other trash isn't the best solution from the standpoint of safety. Perhaps the best compromise is to burn the tampons in a hot fire, making sure they're completely consumed. If not, bag up the charred remains, and pack them out as trash; the odor will be gone and the danger much diminished.

Bear in Mind

Travel into any wildland area always entails risk. Although the practices we've outlined may reduce your chances of a confrontation with a bear, they don't guarantee your safety. An element of risk will always be present, for very little is known for certain about bear behavior in relation to humankind. Like people, bears are intelligent, unpredictable, and capable of inflicting great harm; it is for these reasons we respect them.

One thing seems certain, however. It's time we began thinking from the perspective of this wilderness species before its wildness disappears and we're left with an animal that no longer symbolizes wild country. It is people who have entered into the last strongholds of the bear, not the other way around. Our behavior must reflect our respect and protect bears from us, as much as us from bears.

Grizzly Bear

Will Waterman

A Final Thought

Perhaps the only thing harder than writing a book about ethics is reading one. Wildland users value independence; we don't want anyone suggesting what we should do or how we should act. After all, no one dictated our forebears' behavior toward wilderness. We seek some of that same freedom from society's rules.

Yet how easily we forget that only a short while ago *wilderness* had an entirely different meaning. There were few of us then, and wilderness was something that stood in the way. We fought, cursed, and feared it. Not until recently, with civilization crowding what little wildland remains, did we decide wilderness has other deep-rooted values. As John Muir observed, "Thousands of tired, nerve-shaken, over-civilized people are beginning to find out that going to the mountains is going home: that wildness is a necessity . . ."

Muir's words have come true, beyond his wildest dreams. So much, in fact, that where we once measured human success by the ability to survive wilderness, we must now ask: Can wilderness survive humankind? It may, but marking boundaries and setting aside remote areas are not enough. Nor are regulations imposed by land managers once damage has been done. Those of us who use this land must take responsibility for its health. Aldo Leopold said it best: "Health is the capacity of the land for self-renewal. Conservation is our effort to understand and preserve this capacity."

Exactly how healthy our wildlands will be in the future depends on our behavior every time we hike a trail or canoe a river. If our use is wise, the land won't suffer unduly from our presence, and others may have a similarly unique experience. In this respect, a wildland ethic may be the most important item we carry into the backcountry, as well as the most important lesson we take back home to our everyday lives.

A wildland ethic should not be a burden. It should come naturally, just as concern and responsibility for those whom you love comes as you mature. But first, you must learn about your wildlands and how to travel softly on them. Get experience, preferably from knowledgeable companions or a school offering a qualified outdoor program. It's not enough to read a book, intending to practice minimum-impact techniques on your next trip. Too often, inexperienced visitors find they have to compromise certain practices because the mountain or the river handed them something they were not expecting. Building a fire at timberline because you forgot to bring repair parts for your stove, or losing your food to a bear because you couldn't tie the correct knot to hang it in a tree, isn't practicing a wildland ethic. Plan ahead. Be organized. Anticipate difficulties that may cause you to compromise truly responsible behavior.

Whether you use the backcountry for climbing, fishing, hunting, backpacking, or river running, all wildland recreation should have one objective in common: participation governed by self-conscious restraint. Accepting and following an ethic with the integrity of the land foremost in our minds, we transcend the obvious goal of climbing a summit, catching a five-pound trout, or hiking twenty miles to camp beside an alpine lake. The original goal soon fades, and we are left with the deep satisfaction that comes with rekindling a profound respect for the land.

A sign at the entrance to Tanzania's Manyara National Park, close to where human beings first stood on the edge of the world and saw wilderness everywhere, best sums it up:

Let no one say
and say it to your shame
that all was beauty here
until you came.

Further Reading

Public awareness of human social and environmental impact on wildlands has been slow to emerge from the professional literature written by specialists who study this subject. Even slower to come have been helpful recommendations based on these findings, with the intent of positively influencing visitor behavior. Part of the problem is that this science is relatively new and loosely structured; after all, recreational impact itself has only recently become widespread. But some of the fault must fall on all of us in the environmental community. In our struggle to increase the amount of designated backcountry land, we've been blind to the problems caused by our own use. By ignoring these problems and not encouraging the research that will guide future use, we've been shortsighted. We may secure more wildlands, only to discover they've lost much of their value because of poor stewardship.

With the call for more knowledge about recreational impact, the following list of publications provides source material for readers desiring more information regarding recommendations found in the text.

One The Case for Minimum Impact

Cordell, K. H. and Hendee, J. C.
1980 Renewable resources recreation in the United States: supply, demand, and critical policy issues. American Forestry Association, Washington, D.C. 88 pages.

Frome, M.
1985 *Issues in Wilderness Management.* Westview Press, Boulder, Colorado. 252 pages.

Hammitt, W. E. and Cole, D. N.
1987 *Wildland Recreation: Ecology and Management.* John Wiley and Sons, New York, New York. 341 pages.

Hendee, J. C., Stankey, G. H. and Lucas, R. C.
1978 *Wilderness Management.* Miscellaneous Publication No. 1365. U.S. Department of Agriculture, Forest Service, Washington, D.C. 381 pages.

Washburne, R. F. and Cole, D. N.
1983 Problems and practices in wilderness management: a survey of managers. USDA Forest Service Research Paper INT-304. Intermountain Forest and Range Experiment Station, Ogden, Utah. 56 pages.

Two Backcountry Travel

Boyle, S. A. and Samson, F. B.
1985 Effects of nonconsumptive recreation on wildlife: a review. *Wildlife Society Bulletin.* 13:110–116.

Harlow, W. M.
1977 Stop walking away the wilderness. *Backpacker.* 5(4):33–36.

Lucas, R. C.
1980 Use patterns and visitor characteristics, attitudes and preferences in nine wilderness and other roadless areas. USDA Forest Service Research Paper INT-253. Intermountain Forest and Range Experiment Station, Ogden, Utah. 89 pages.

Turner, T.
1986 Rush Hour in the National Forests. *Sierra.* 71(3):26–28.

Three Selecting and Using a Campsite

Brown, P. J. and Schomaker, J. H.
1974 Final report on criteria for potential wilderness campsites. USDA Forest Service Intermountain Forest and Range Experiment Station, Missoula, Montana. 50 pages.

Cole, D. N.
1981 Vegetational changes associated with recreational use and fire suppression in the Eagle Cap Wilderness, Oregon: some management implications. *Biological Conservation.* 20:247–270.

Cole, D. N.
1982 Controlling the spread of campsites at popular wilderness destinations. *Journal of Soil & Water Conservation.* 37:291–295.

Cole, N. N.
1987 Research on soil and vegetation in wilderness: a state-of-knowledge review. Proceedings—National Wilderness Research Conference: Issues, State-of-knowledge, Future Directions. USDA Forest Service General Technical Report INT-220. Intermountain Research Station, Ogden, Utah. Pages 135–177.

Cole, N. N. and Benedict, J.
1983 Wilderness campsite selection—what should users be told? *Park Science.* 3(4): 5–7.

Cole, D. N. and Fichtler, R. K.
1983 Campsite impact and frequency of use in three western wilderness areas. *Environmental Management.* 7:275–288.

Frissell, S. S. and Duncan, D. P.
1965 Campsite preference and deterioration in the Quetico-Superior canoe country. *Journal of Forestry.* 63:256–260.

Merriam, L. C., Jr. and Smith, C. K.
1974 Visitor impact on newly developed campsites in the Boundary Waters Canoe Area. *Journal of Forestry.* 72:627–630.

Stankey, G. H.
1973 Visitor perception of wilderness recreation carrying capacity. USDA Forest Service Research Paper INT-142. Intermountain Forest

and Range Experiment Station, Ogden, Utah. 61 pages.

Four Fires and Stoves

Cole, D. N. and Dalle-Molle, J.
1982 Managing campfire impacts in the back-country. USDA Forest Service General Technical Report INT-135. Intermountain Forest and Range Experiment Station, Ogden, Utah. 16 pages.

Fenn, D. B., Gogue, G. J. and Burge, R. E.
1976 Effects of campfires on soil properties. National Park Service Ecological Service Bulletin No. 5. Washington, D.C. 16 pages.

Harvey, H. T., Hartesveldt, R. J. and Stanley, J. T.
1972 *Wilderness Impact Study Report.* Sierra Club Outing Committee, Palo Alto, California. 87 pages.

Harvey, A. E., Jurgensen, M. and Larsen, M. J.
1979 Role of forest fuels in the biology and management of soil. USDA Forest Service Research Paper INT-65. Intermountain Forest and Range Experiment Station, Ogden, Utah. 8 pages.

Five Sanitation and Waste Disposal

Silverman, G. and Erman, D. C.
1979 Alpine lakes in Kings Canyon National Park, California: baseline conditions and possible effects of visitor use. *Journal of Environmental Management.* 8:73–87.

Stanley, J. T., Harvey, H. T. and Hartesveldt, R. J.
1979 *Wilderness Impact Study.* Sierra Club Outing Committee, Palo Alto, California. 290 pages.

Suk, T. J., Riggs, J. L. and Nelson, B. C.
1986 Water contamination with *Giardia* in back-country areas. Proceedings—National Wilderness Research Conference: Current Research. USDA Forest Service General Technical Report INT-212. Intermountain Research Station, Ogden, Utah. Pages 237–244.

Temple, K. L., Camper, A. K. and Lucas, R. C.
1982 Potential health hazard from human waste in wilderness. *Journal of Soil and Water Conservation.* 37:357–359.

Six Deserts

Cole, D. N.
1985 Ecological impacts on backcountry campsites in Grand Canyon National Park, Arizona, USA. *Journal of Environmental Management.* 10(5):651–659.

Seven Rivers and Lakes

Carothers, S. W., Johnson, R. A. and Dolan, R.
1984 Recreational impacts on Colorado River beaches in Glen Canyon, Arizona. *Environmental Management.* 8:353–360.

Cordell, K. H. and Hendee, J. C.
1980 Renewable resources recreation in the United States: supply, demand, and critical policy issues. American Forestry Association, Washington, D.C. 88 pages.

Zaslowsky, D.
1986 *These American Lands.* Henry Holt and Company, Inc., New York, New York. 404 pages.

Eight Coasts

Baker, C. S., Herman, L. M., Bays, B. G. and Bauer, G. B.
1983 The impact of vessel traffic on the behavior of humpback whales. Proceedings—First Glacier Bay Science Symposium. USDI, Science Publications Office, Atlanta, Georgia. Page 54.

Godfrey, P. J. and Godfrey, M. M.
1980 Ecological effects of off-road vehicles on Cape Code. *Oceanus.* 23(4):56–66.

Nine Alpine and Arctic Tundra

Cooper, D. J.
1985 The Arrigetch Peaks region of the central Brooks Range, Alaska: ecosystems and human use. Proceedings—National Wilderness Research Conference: Current Research. USDA Forest Service General Technical Report INT-212. Intermountain Research Station, Ogden, Utah. Pages 94–99.

Edwards, O. M.
1979 Vegetation disturbance by natural factors and visitor impact in the alpine zone of Mt. Rainier National Park: implications for management. Proceedings—Recreation Impact on Wildlands Conference. USDA Forest Service, Pacific Northwest Region, Portland, Oregon. R-6-001-1979. Pages 101–108.

Hartley, E. A.
1976 Man's effects on the stability of alpine and subalpine vegetation in Glacier National Park, Montana. Ph.D. dissertation. Duke University, Durham, North Carolina. 258 pages.

Hendee, J. C., Clark, R. N. and Dailey, T.
1974 Fishing and other recreation behavior at high mountain lakes. USDA Forest Service Research Note PNW-304. Pacific Northwest Forest and Range Experiment Station, Portland, Oregon. 14 pages.

Price, M. F.
1985 Impacts of recreational activities on alpine vegetation in Western North America. *Mountain Research and Development.* 5(3):263–277.

Silverman, G. and Erman, D. C.
1979 Alpine lakes in Kings Canyon National Park, California: baseline conditions and possible effects of visitor use. *Journal of Environmental Management.* 8:73–87.

Willard, B. E. and Marr, J. W.
1971 Recovery of alpine tundra under protection after damage by human activities in the Rocky Mountains of Colorado. *Biological Conservation.* 3:181–190.

Ten Snow and Ice

Ferguson, M. A. and Keith, L. B.
1982 Influence of Nordic skiing on distribution of moose and elk in Elk Island National Park, Alberta. *Canadian Field-Naturalist.* 96: 69–78.

Hammitt, W. E., McDonald, C. D. and Hughes, J. L.
1985 Experience level and participation motives of winter wilderness users. Proceedings—National Wilderness Research Conference: Current Research. USDA Forest Service General Technical Report INT-212. Intermountain Research Station, Ogden, Utah. Pages 269–277.

Eleven Bear Country

Cushing, B.
1983 Responses of polar bears to human menstrual odors. Proceedings—Fifth International Conference on Bear Research and Management, International Association for Bear Research and Management. Pages 275–280.

Herrero, S.
1985 *Bear Attacks: Their Causes and Avoidance.* Winchester Press, Piscataway, New Jersey. 287 pages.

Schneider, B.
1977 *Where the Grizzly Walks.* Moutain Press Publishing Co., Missoula, Montana. 191 pages.

Servheen, C.
1985 Biological requirements of a wilderness species. Proceedings—National Wilderness Research Conference: Current Research. USDA Forest Service General Technical Report INT-212. Intermountain Research Station, Ogden, Utah. Pages 173–175.

Design and Graphic Production
by Art Unlimited